ROBERTO BARTOLINI

**W9-COJ-418**

COMPLETE GUIDE OF

# FLORENCE

### and its hills

*USEFUL INFORMATION*

*New edition of the "Practical Guide"*
*up-dated according to the latest rearrangements*
*of the Galleries and Museums*

NOVA LVX

Publishing House Becocci
Largo Liverani, 12/3 Florence

*Tuscany is decorated with Florence like a ring
with an expensive jewel; and the town is adorned
with all sorts of good things, like a virginal neck
with a beautiful necklace.*
G. Dati, *La sfera*

**Florence as it was**

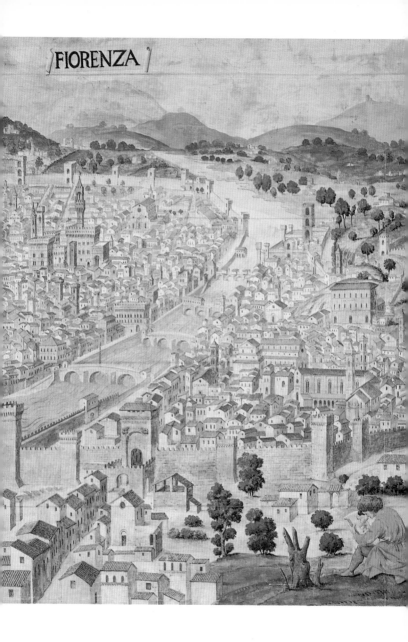

FIORENZA

# GENERAL INDEX

## ITINERARIES

I.   Piazza della Signoria, page 18; Loggia della Signoria, page 19 - Palazzo Vecchio, page 21 - Palace of the Uffizi, page 33 - Uffizi Gallery, page 34 - Church of Orsanmichele, page 81 - Piazza Duomo, Baptistry, page 86 - Cathedral (S. Maria del Fiore), page 91 - Giotto's bell-tower, page 97 - Museum of the Opera del Duomo, page 99.

II.  Square and Church of San Lorenzo, page 101 - Laurentian Library, page 105 - Medici Chapels, page 106 - Medici-Riccardi Palace, page 111 - Square and Church of San Marco, page 114 - Museum of S. Marco (Angelico), page 115 - Academy Gallery (Tribune of David), page 123.

III. Piazza della Repubblica - Straw Market - Ponte Vecchio, page 127 - Pitti Palace, page 130 - Palatine Gallery, page 134 - Royal Apartments, page 139 - Museum of Silverware, page 148 - Boboli Gardens, page 151 - Gallery of Modern Art, page 155 - Square and Church of S. Spirito, page 158 - Church of the Carmine, page 160.

IV. Square and Church of S. Firenze, Bargello, page 165 - National Museum, page 167 - Church of the Badia Fiorentina, page 175 - House of Dante, page 178 - Piazza S. Croce, page 179 - Church of S. Croce, page 180 - Cloister of S. Croce page, 190 - Museum of Opera di S. Croce, page 191 - Pazzi Chapel, page 192 - Casa Buonarroti, page 194.

## EXCURSIONS

## LESS FREQUENTED MUSEUMS, THAT MERIT BEING VISITED

# Principal Churches, Galleries, Museums and Palaces in alphabetical order

8

# HISTORICAL-ARTISTIC BACKGROUND

The origin of Florence goes back to the period of the Etruscan civilization. According to some historians, the Etruscans of Fiesole were the first to settle in the Arno valley. Later the Romans, after the war of Sulla, occupied this fertile location, and Caesar's veterans founded, on the banks of the river, the colony with the auspicious name of "Florentia" (I cent. BC). St. Miniato, who brought Christianity to Florence, was here martyred in the III century. During the barbaric invasions, Florence suffered the harsh times of the other Italian cities. In 1115, after having weakened the feudal Lords, the Florentine people formed a free Commune.

After nearby Fiesole was conquered (1125), a second circle of walls was built around Florence, since the first was now insufficient.

From the XII to the XVI centuries, Florence aesthetically acquires that physiognomy that she still maintains, characterized by the classical sense of proportion and the chromatic marble decoration.

In architecture, this first period is exemplified by the *Church of San Miniato* and the *Baptistry,* while in sculpture, the *Pulpit* of *San Miniato* (1207) is the most notable example. In art, the great personalities of Cimabue and Giotto stand out and Dante becomes an important literary figure. At the end of the XIII cent. three important churches are erected: *Santa Maria Novella* for the Dominicans, *Santa Croce* for the Franciscans and the *Cathedral,* testimony to how Northern linearism is transformed in vast spaces with vigorously conceived monumental forms.

Together with religious architecture, civilian construction develops, the most notable examples being: the *Palace of the Bargello,* the *Palazzo Vecchio* and the *Loggia of the Signoria,* called of the *Lanzi.*

With Dante (1265-1321) and *Giotto* (1266-1337), Florence begins her glorious era in culture and art. In the school of *Arnolfo di Cambio* 1204-1302) and that of Giotto, Andrea Pisano da Pontedera (1295-1345), author of the first Baptistry gates, forms his style.

*Cimabue* (1240-1302) surpasses the Byzantine formulas still loitering in Florence. *Giotto,* his great pupil, frees Florentine art from all its ties with the past, introducing to art, especially painting, a new human language, rendered with profound and attentive observation. From Giotto derive *Taddeo Gaddi, Bernardo Daddi, Masi di Banco* and many others.

The great XIV century artists announce the coming of the XV century, glorious period of the "Renaissance" (rebirth) during which time Florence re-lives the illustrious era that Athens knew in ancient Greece.

*Filippo Brunelleschi* (1377-1446), architect, erects constructions based on a new conception of proportion and volume derived from classic art.

*Donatello* (1386-1466), friend and collaborator of Brunelleschi, freeing sculpture from all Gothic influence, creates his masterpieces, rich with profound humanity due to his attentive observation of nature.

*Masaccio* (1401-1428), despite his brief lifetime, inspired by Donatello and above all Brunelleschi, introduces new elements of perspective and color in his creations that make him the first "Renaissance" painter. His frescoes in the *Carmine Church,* monumentally figurative in their powerful humanity, open new and more vast horizons to Italian art.

*Leon Battista Alberti* (1404-1472), musician, painter and author of art treatises, is the theoretical head of Florentine architecture. *Michelozzo* (1396-1472) is the architect of the *Medici-Riccardi Palace; Benedetto da Maiano* of the *Strozzi Palace; Lorenzo Ghiberti* (1378-1455) goldsmith, architect and sculptor, enriches the Baptistry with his famous doors. Students and followers of Donatello continue more or less near to his style of art. Among these: *Bertoldo* (1420-1492), *Desiderio da Settignano* (1428-1464), *Mino da Fiesole* (1430-1484), and *Luca della Robbia* (1408-1482), Andrea, his nephew, and Giovanni, Andrea's son, who, with their terracotta works of art represent the most popular and widespread figurative aspect of the Renaissance.

Inspired by Brunelleschi, Donatello and Masaccio are: *Andrea del Castagno* (1423-1457) who painted dramatic and realistic creations; *Paolo Uccello* (1397-1475), creator of perspective and volume; *Domenico Veneziano* who endows his work with natural light; *Filippo Lippi* who reconciles Masaccio's principles with Donatello's synthetic line. After the middle of the XV century, *Antonio del Pollaiolo* (1432-98) and *Botticelli* (1445-1510), artists of different temperaments, with their vibrant lines that generate volumes, elevate Florentine Renaissance art to higher levels.

At the end of the XV century, when the representatives of the first generation of Renaissance art have died out, *Leonardo* (1452-1519) and *Michelangelo* (1475-1564) appear on the horizon. The atmosphere of ultra-sensitive light and shadow that bathes the pictorial vision, called "sfumato", of the former finds its correspondent in the dramatic and vehement "non-finito" (unfinished) of the latter, who leads architecture, sculpture and painting to the highest summits of the Renaissance.

With the fall of the Florentine Republic, Michelangelo, valiant defender of the city, leaves Florence profoundly embittered and goes to Rome where he dies. His body is brought back to Florence and buried in St. Croce. Also Leonardo, who had already left Florence and lived for a while in Milan, goes to France where he dies and is buried in Amboise.

In the 16th century Florence is still an active center of schools of art, the most important of which is that of the so-called "mannerists", creators of sensitive technical refinements. Among the most famous painters are: *Rosso Fiorentino, Pontormo* and *Bronzino. In sculpture we remember Giambologna* and *Cellini* (also a great goldsmith). In architecture: *Vasari, Ammannati* and *Buontalenti.*

In the XVII century Florentine art becomes provincial, even though artists such as *Giovanni da San Giovanni, Furini* and *Stefano della Bella* are worthy of consideration.

The XIX century, after a period of academic controversies between classicists and romanticists, is punctualized by the artistic movement of the "Macchiaioli", among whom excel *Fattori* and *Signorini.* The splendid Tuscan country-side, the enchantment of the Arno, and the melody of the olive groves, are rendered chromatically by means of the "macchia" (spots of color), painting that can be considered, although on a provincial level, the Italian correspondent of the celebrated French Impressionism.

Reopening the brief historical background previously outlined up to 1125, despite the bloody fighting between the Guelphs and Ghibellines (the former backed by the Pope, the latter by the Emperor), Florence becomes wealthier because of the great expansion of her commerce, especially the wood and silk industries. In order to impede the export of secondary products the Tribunale di Mercanzia (Commercial Court) was created. No one could take part in the city government if he did not belong to one of the famous guilds. In order to partecipate in the government, Dante became a member of the Doctors and Apothacaries Guild.

With the crushing victory of the *Guelphs* over the *Ghibellines* (1267), the "Government of the Signori and Priori" is created.

The struggles continue: the Guelphs split into *Bianchi* (whites) and *Neri* (blacks). Dante, who is a White, is exiled from the city, and, after having wandered around France and Italy, dies and is buried in Ravenna in 1321. Despite the furious internal fighting, the cities commerce continues to grow, even though the plaque of 1348 decimates her population from 90,000 to 30,000 inhabitants.

The Lombard money lenders are succeeded by the great Florentine bankers under the patronage of St. Matthew. Because of their ability and honesty, they become so influential that Popes and Sovereigns turn

**Fig. 2 - St. Croce quarter during the flood of November 4, 1966**

# GENEALOGICAL TREE OF THE MEDICI

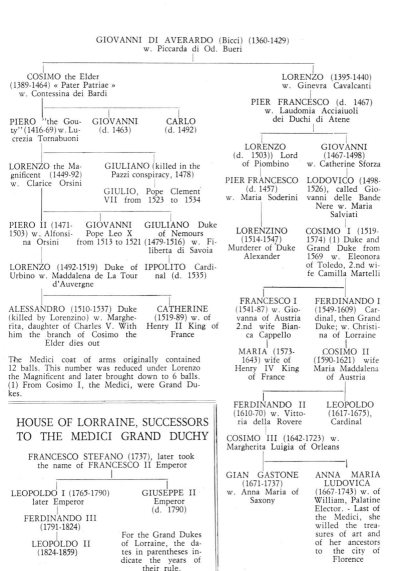

GIOVANNI DI AVERARDO (Bicci) (1360-1429)
w. Piccarda di Od. Bueri

COSIMO the Elder
(1389-1464) « Pater Patriae »
w. Contessina dei Bardi

LORENZO (1395-1440)
w. Ginevra Cavalcanti

PIER FRANCESCO (d. 1467)
w. Laudomia Acciaiuoli
dei Duchi di Atene

PIERO ''the Gou-
ty'' (1416-69) w. Lu-
crezia Tornabuoni

GIOVANNI
(d. 1463)

CARLO
(d. 1492)

LORENZO
(d. 1503)) Lord
of Piombino

GIOVANNI
(1467-1498)
w. Catherine Sforza

LORENZO the Ma-
gnificent (1449-92)
w. Clarice Orsini

GIULIANO (killed in the
Pazzi conspiracy, 1478)

GIULIO, Pope Clement
VII from 1523 to 1534

PIER FRANCESCO
(d. 1457)
w. Maria Soderini

LODOVICO (1498-
1526), called Gio-
vanni delle Bande
Nere w. Maria
Salviati

PIERO II (1471-
1503) w. Alfonsi-
na Orsini

GIOVANNI
Pope Leo X
from 1513 to 1521

GIULIANO Duke
of Nemours
(1479-1516) w. Fi-
liberta di Savoia

LORENZINO
(1514-1547)
Murderer of Duke
Alexander

COSIMO I (1519-
1574) (1) Duke and
Grand Duke from
1569 w. Eleonora
of Toledo, 2.nd wi-
fe Camilla Martelli

LORENZO (1492-1519) Duke of
Urbino w. Maddalena de La Tour
d'Auvergne

IPPOLITO Cardi-
nal (d. 1535)

ALESSANDRO (1510-1537) Duke
(killed by Lorenzino) w. Margherita, daughter of Charles V. With
him the branch of Cosimo the
Elder dies out

CATHERINE
(1519-89) w. of
Henry II King of
France

FRANCESCO I
(1541-87) w. Gio-
vanna of Austria
2.nd wife Bian-
ca Cappello

FERDINANDO I
(1549-1609) Car-
dinal, then Grand
Duke; w. Christi-
na of Lorraine

The Medici coat of arms originally contained
12 balls. This number was reduced under Lorenzo
the Magnificent and later brought down to 6 balls.
(1) From Cosimo I, the Medici, were Grand Dukes.

MARIA (1573-
1643) wife of
Henry IV King
of France

COSIMO II
(1590-1621) wife
Maria Maddalena
of Austria

FERDINANDO II
(1610-70) w. Vitto-
ria della Rovere

LEOPOLDO
(1617-1675),
Cardinal

## HOUSE OF LORRAINE, SUCCESSORS TO THE MEDICI GRAND DUCHY

COSIMO III (1642-1723) w.
Margherita Luigia of Orleans

FRANCESCO STEFANO (1737), later took
the name of FRANCESCO II Emperor

GIAN GASTONE
(1671-1737)
w. Anna Maria of
Saxony

ANNA MARIA
LUDOVICA
(1667-1743) w. of
William, Palatine
Elector. - Last of
the Medici, she
willed the trea-
sures of art and
of her ancestors
to the city of
Florence

LEOPOLDO I (1765-1790)
later Emperor

GIUSEPPE II
Emperor
(d. 1790)

FERDINANDO III
(1791-1824)

LEOPOLDO II
(1824-1859)

For the Grand Dukes
of Lorraine, the da-
tes in parentheses in-
dicate the years of
their rule.

to them for large loans, even choosing them as their treasurers.

The financial and banking center was the *Piazza of the Mercato Nuovo* (today called "straw market" or "Porcellino"), at that time without the portico. The financial transactions took place on 80 rug covered tables, on which were placed sacks full of gold "florins", the Florentine currency that was prized in all of Europe. Here, where the schedules of the port of Leghorn were also displayed, nobody who was armed was allowed to take part in the operations. Among the Florentine bankers, the Medici were the most powerful. Cosimo called *"the Elder"* (1389-1464), was the successor in the bank of his father Giovanni, gonfalonier of the city. The founder of a new banking system, he accumulates so much wealth, that he becomes the most influential man in the city government. He was hindered with every means by dangerous adversaries, among whom was Rinaldo degli Albizi who, unable to suppress him, had him exiled to Venice for ten years, where he further extends his financial empire. Because of his many influential acquaintances he shortens his exile, returns the following year acclaimed "Gentleman (Signore) of the city", and succeeds in driving his powerful enemies out of Florence. In order to avoid arousing jealousies Cosimo lives like a private citizen, however, placing the city in the hands of 70 faithful followers who govern for him. He is careful to protect the monastic orders who have such great influence on the people. Under his patronage, the Greek and Roman Churches meet at the Council of Florence (1439). Well known patron and prudent governor, he was honored with the title "Father of his Country". Cosimo's mediocre son *Piero,* called "the Gouty" who dies in 1469 of this illness, is succeeded by his grandson *Lorenzo.* He is in no way hindered by his powerful adversaries who felt that, because he was so young, he would commit inevitable and irreparable errors that would automatically cause his removal from the government. But Lorenzo, having been prepared by his mother Lucrezia Tornabuoni, governed Florence with such wisdom that he merited the title "Magnificent". From near and far his rivals prepared a conspiracy, headed by the Pazzi, which took place in the Cathedral on Easter morning 1478, where Lorenzo saves himself in the sacristy while Giuliano falls under the knives of the conspirators. Lorenzo, who now remains the only descendent of this great family, by avoiding any bloodshed to revenge his brother Giuliano, becomes even more popular. He wisely takes advantage of this sad situation to more easily get rid of his powerful enemies, thus becoming absolute heir, arbitrater of the city, and most prestigious man of the era. Heads of other Italian states turn to him for advice. Under Lorenzo, Florence lives the most glorious years of art and culture. Lorenzo's son Giovanni, young and brilliant Cardinal, becomes Pope Leo X (1513-21) and appoints many of his faithful followers to the office of Cardinal, thus preparing the Papacy for his cousin Cardinal Giulio (son of Giuliano assassinated in the Cathedral) who becomes Pope Clement VII (1523-32). Entering in the sphere of the Great European families, the Medici give two famous queens to France: *Catherine,* wife of Henry II and *Maria,* of Henry IV.

Upon the death of Lorenzo the Medici power seems to fall apart. Charles VIII of France enters Florence and Lorenzo's son Piero flees scorned by his countrymen. *Pier Capponi* becomes the arbitrator of the city and, threatening to "ring the bells" to call the people to arms to defend the city, he obliges the invading king to leave Florence (1494), which becomes a Republic once again.

*Savanarola* becomes head of the Republic. His ardent mission as a reformer places him against the powerful who, through intrigues, have him hanged and burned in Signoria Square with his followers Maruffi and Buonvicini (May 23, 1498).

The Medici return stronger than ever. The last dream of the Florentines to live in a free Republic vanishes after the memorable seige and heroic sacrifice of *Francesco Ferrucci* (1529) the champion of Florentine patriots. *Alexander Medici,* with the support of Charles V and Pope Clement VII (his relative), becomes the first Duke of the city. Revealing himself a tyrant, he is killed by his cousin *Lorenzino* (1537). With the slaying of Alexander ends the branch of Cosimo the Elder and the second branch of the Medici begins (as illustrated in the enclosed genealogical tree of the Medici). *Cosimo I* (1519-1574), son of Giovanni delle Bande Nere (famous soldier) becomes absolute ruler of the city, and, from 1569, Grand Duke of Florence and Tuscany.

Cosimo I's successors soon become secondary figures in a vaster political and economic world. *Anna Maria Ludovica* (1667-1743), called "Electress Palatine", with the "Family Pact" drawn up in Vienna (1737), specifies that all the art treasures collected by her family are to remain in Florence to be forever enjoyed by the Florentines and the world. Thanks to this generous legacy, all the works of art taken during the last war were able to be recuperated.

After the Medici, Tuscany is ruled by the Dukes of Lorraine who are driven out in 1859. From 1865 to 1871 Florence was the capitol of the kingdom of Italy.

# FIRST ITINERARY

*Piazza della Signoria — Loggia della Signoria (dei Lanzi) — Palazzo Vecchio — Uffizi Gallery — Church of Orsanmichele — Via Calzaiuoli — Loggia del Bigallo — Piazza Duomo — Baptistry — Cathedral (Santa Maria del Fiore ) — Bell Tower — Oratory of the Misericordia — Museum of the Opera del Duomo.* (This itinerary is indicated by the numbers 10, 9, 2, 3 of the monumental map.)

## PIAZZA DELLA SIGNORIA (Fig. 3)

Hearth of the origin and of the history of the Florentine Republic, the square still conserves its character as the political center of the city.

The square is dominated by the XIV century Palazzo Vecchio with the bold crenellated tower (fig. 3). On the right we can see the Uffizi Gallery and the Loggia della Signoria. On the left, at the end of the square: the Palace of the Tribunale della Mercanzia (Commercial Court) now the Bureau of Agriculture; to the left, at no. 7, the Uguccioni Palace, by Folfi (1549), with a bust of Cosimo I in the niche. In front of the Palazzo Vecchio is the Palace of the Assicurazioni Generali, by Landi (1871), whose much discussed imitation of the XV century architecture alters the characteristic basic unity of the Square. Beginning our look at the statues in the square, from left to right we observe: *the bronze equestrian statue of Cosimo I* by Giambologna (1594 - fig. 4) with *episodes of his reign* on the reliefs. Next follows the large *Fountain of Neptune* called by the Florentines "Biancone" (fig. 4) by Ammannati. The base of the fountain has interesting bronze figures of *nymphs and satyrs,* by collaborators of Ammannati, among whom was Giambologna. Near the center of the square a porphyry plaque commemorates the site where Savonarola and his followers Maruffi and Buonvicini were hanged and burned at the stake (25-3-1498). On the steps of the Palazzo Vecchio: *Lion* called "il Marzocco" (fig. 4) with the *Florentine Lily,* a copy of an original by Donatello in the National Museum. On the granite pedestal, *Judith slaying Holofernes* (fig. 4) in bronze, a dramatic work of Donatello's maturity. Near the entrance of the Palace, copy of *David* that substitutes the original by Michelangelo, conserved in the Gallery of the Academy of Fine Arts (Via Ricasoli 60). Followed by the heavy marble group of *Hercules and Cacus, by Bandinelli (1533). At the entrance of the Palace the two statues at one time served to hold the chains that blocked the door. The female statue on the right is by Bandinelli while the male on the left is by Vincenzo de'Rossi. Above the door of the Palace, the monogram between the two Lions* reads: *Christ, King of the City.*

**Loggia della Signoria.** Called erroneously "dell'Orcagna" because at one time it was thought to be by this artist; called also dei Lanzi, because of the Swiss body-guards at the service of Cosimo who took cover here. Now we know that it was built by Benci di Cione and Simone Talenti (1376-82), for the investiture of the Priori and other celebrations of the Republic. It is a notable example of Florentine Gothic architecture, with the wide arches supported by solid pilasters that preludes to the Renaissance.

Above the arches are exquisite lobed panels with figures of the Virtues on a blue enamelled background carved from designs by Agnolo Gaddi. The splendid *Loggia* terminates on high with the vast panoramic terrace.

Under the Loggia: the famous Perseus holding the head of Medusa in bronze by Cellini (fig. 4). In the niches on the base are exquisite sculptures of *mythological figures* in which we see the artist's extraordinary ability as a sculptor and goldsmith together. Copies of the originals kept in the Bargello, just as the bas-relief, representing *Perseus freeing Andromeda.* (On the back of Perseus's head, the semblance of a human face can be detected. This is thought to be Cellini's self-portrait.)

On the steps of the Loggia are two statues of lions, the one on the right

Fig. 4 - Sculpture in Signoria Square: I) Menelaus supporting the body of Patroclus; II) Giambologna: Rape of the Sabine Women; III) Ammannati: Fountain of Neptune; IV) Lion called the "Marzocco"; V Cellini: Perseus; VI) Donatello: Judith slaying Holofernes (copy original inside the Palazzo Vecchio); VII) Giambologna: Hercules fighting the Centaur; VIII) Pio Fedi: Rape of Polixena.

from the classical era and the one on the left is by Vacca (XVI cent.).

Under the right arch of the Loggia is the *Rape of the Sabine Women* (fig.4), the famous marble group by Giambologna, with the same subject represented in bronze on the base.

In the second row the statues are from left to right; *the Rape of Polixena* by Pio Fedi (1886 - fig. 4); *Menelaus supporting the body of Patroclus* (fig. 4): *Hercules fighting the Centaur Nessus* (fig. 4).

Against the wall of the splendid Loggia are six restored antique statues, the third from the left of which is the most notable.

## PALAZZO VECCHIO

The Palazzo Vecchio is attributed to Arnolfo di Cambio who began it in 1299, incorporating the ancient tower of the Foraboschi into its construction. After the death of Arnolfo in 1302, the palace was finished by other artists in 1314. The solid cubical shaped building is enriched by the thrust of the simple tower with its precious Lederle clock which terminates on high with the bell-tower surmounted by the cusp and the lively lion rampant.

In this public palace built as the seat of the Priori, later lived the Duke of Athens, who was driven out because of his tyranny. From 1540 to 1550 it was the home of Cosimo I who enlarged the construction. When Cosimo moved to the Pitti Palace this palace was identified with the name "vecchio" (old) to distinguish it from the new (Pitti) and this name remained. From Via Gondi the additions of the Palazzo Vecchio, executed in the XVI and XVII centuries, are clearly visible. The entrance is here, to correspond with the second courtyard.

**First Courtyard** (fig. 5) remodelled in 1470 by Michelozzo. On high, around the courtyard are crests of the Church, City and the Guilds. In the center, the porphyry fountain with the lively winged boy, a copy of the original by Verrocchio now on the second floor. The columns, at one time smooth, were decorated with colored stucco designs in the XVI century. The frescoes on the walls, representing scenes of Austrian cities, were painted for the wedding of Francesco (son of Cosimo I) and Johanna of Austria. In the niche, *Samson and a Philistine* by Pierino da Vinci. In the corner on the left is the old *Armory,* conserved in its original style and used for temporary exhibitions.

**Second Courtyard,** observe the massive pillars built in 1494 to sustain the great *Salone dei Cinquecento* on the second floor.

**Third Courtyard,** is used as City Council offices. Between the first and second courtyard, the monumental staircase by Vasari leads to the

**Salone dei Cinquecento** (fig. 6). It was built in 1494 by Simone del Pol laiolo, called "il Cronaca", on commission of Savonarola who, becoming spiritual leader of the Republic after the exile of the Medici, wanted it as the seat of the Grand Council consisting of 500 members. Later under Cosimo I, the Hall was enlarged by Vasari. During this trans formation famous works were lost including the cartoons of the "battle of Anghiari" by Leonardo and that of the "battle of Cascina" by Miche langelo, with which the two artists were supposed to decorate the walls of the room. Among the historic events which took place in this hall we remember the proclamation of the adherence of Tuscany to the Kin gdom of Italy (1859). From 1865 to 1871, when Florence was the capita of Italy, the representatives held their meeetings here. Now congresses concerts and other public manifestations are held here. On the walls are enormous and pompous frescoes by Vasari and helpers (1550 1570), that represent, beginning with the wall opposite to the entrance from left to right: 1) *The taking of Siena* (fig. 7); 2) *The Conquest of Porto Ercole;* 3) *Victory of Cosimo I at Marciano in Val di Chiana.* On the entrance wall, from left to right: 1) *Defeat of the Pisans at the Tower of S. Vincenzo;* 2) *Maximillian of Austria attempts the conquest of Leghorn;* 3) *Pisa attacked by the Florentine troops.* The ceiling is made up of 34 panels also by Vasari and followers representing *episodes from the life of Cosimo I,* culminating in the center with the *scene of his glorification as Grand Duke of Florence and Tuscany.*

On the north side of the Hall, illuminated by enormous windows, is the raised stage called the "Udienza", built by Cosimo I to receive citizens and ambassadors. Above are frescoes of historical episodes; among these, on the left, that of Boniface VIII receiving the ambassadors of foreign States and, seeing that they were all Florentines pronounces the famous words, "You Florentines are the quintessence". In the niches are sculptures, by Bandinelli: in the center, that *of Leo X*; on the right *Charles V crowned by Clement VII.*

On the left, entrance to the vestibule that leads to the splendid "Salone dei Duecento", closed to the public because it is reserved for city func tions.

Continuing in the Salone dei Cinquecento, along the walls we can admire valuable Medicean tapestries with *Stories of the life of St. John the Baptist,* taken from the frescoes by Andrea del Sarto. The statues that represent the *Labors of Hercules* are by Vincenzo de' Rossi, pupil

Fig. 5 - Palazzo Vecchio - Fountain of the first courtyard

**Fig. 6 - Palazzo Vecchio - Salone dei Cinquecento (Hall of the Five Hundred)**

of Bandinelli. In the centre, facing the entrance is Michelangelo's famous *Victory* (fig. 8), designed for the tomb of Julius II, representing the triumph of virtue over vice. It was given the name Victory in 1921 when it was brought here from the Bargello Museum to celebrate the victory of World War I.

On the right, through the glass door, we enter the *Small study-room (studiolo) of Francesco I Medici* (fig. 9), who was an expert in alchemy and had this small laboratory built for himself by Vasari (1570). It is a charming rectangular shaped room with a barrel vaulted ceiling frescoed by Poppi with *allegories of Prometheus and the Elements.* In the Lunettes are portraits of *Cosimo I and his wife Eleonor of Toledo* by Bronzino. Among the gracious sculptures is the *"Apollino"* by Giambologna. On the cabinet doors are interesting paintings of the mysteries of alchemy and other mythological episodes, by Alessandro Allori, Cavalori, Macchietti and other artists of the late XVI century. Opening the door to the left at the back of the room, we climb to the secret archives from where we go down to the small treasure room reserved (it is believed) for the valuables of Cosimo I. Going back to the Studiolo, we return to the Salone dei Cinquecento. Through the glass door on the right of the opposite wall we climb to the "Hall of Leo X" (now the mayor's waiting room) frescoed by Vasari with episodes from the life of

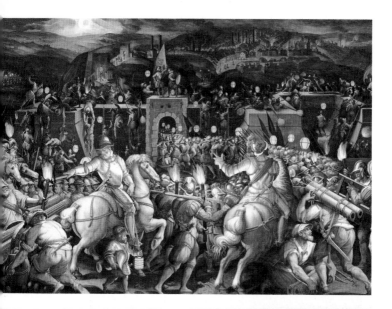

Fig. 7 - Salone dei Cinquecento - Vasari: Conquest of Siena
Fig. 8 - Salone dei Cinquecento - Michelangelo: Victory
Fig. 9 - Studiolo of Francesco I of the Medici

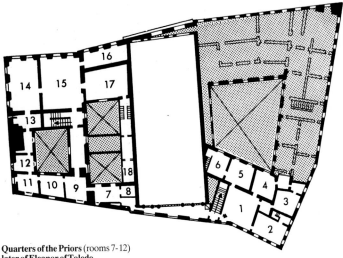

**Quarters of the Priors** (rooms 7-12)
later of Eleanor of Toledo
wife of Cosimo I

13. Chapel of the Signoria
14. Sala delle Udienze or Hall of Justice
15. Room of the Lilies
16. Old Chancellery
17. Cloakroom
18. Study room

**Apartments of the Elements**

1. Room of the Elements
2. Terrace of Saturn
3. Hercules Room
4. Room of Jupiter
5. Room of Cybele
6. Ceres room

this Medici Pope. To the left of the fireplace is the Chapel that contains the copy of Raphael's *Madonna dell'Impannata* (the original is in the Pitti Palace). On the sides are frescoes of *SS. Cosmos and Damian* patron saints of the Medici, in the semblance of Cosimo the Elder and Cosimo I. On the right are other rooms of historical interest reserved for the mayor's offices. In order to avoid the steep staircase that leads to the third floor it is advisable to take the elevator which can be found in the Salone.

**Second Floor.** Leaving the elevator, in the vestibule to the left (as shown on the plan), after having observed the steep staircase with the vault decorated with grotesques, we enter the rooms called the

**Apartments of the Elements** decorated by Vasari and helpers, representing on the walls in the First Room (fig. 10), *Allegories of Water, Fire and Earth* and, on the ceiling, that of *Saturn*. Opening the door in front we pass into the

**Fig. 10 - Palazzo Vecchio - Sala degli Elementi (Apartment of the Elements)**

**Terrace of Saturn,** so called because of the ceiling motif, with its splendid Florentine roof. In the corner , the gracious little bronze devil by Giambologna (that one time decorated a corner of the Sassetti Palace). From here we can admire the façade of S. Croce; on the right of the Arno, Piazzale Michelangelo, S. Miniato, and, farther right the Fortress Belvedere. Looking down to the right, can be seen remains of the Church of S. Pietro Scheraggio incorporated into the Uffizi, and above, the passageway that joins the Uffizi to the Pitti Palace passing over the Ponte Vecchio. To the left is the Hercules Room that gets its name from the subject of the paintings on the ceiling. Also the tapestry has stories of Hercules. The room contains a *Madonna and Child* (Florentine school of the XVI cent.) and a valuable ebony cabinet *(stipo)* inlaid with semi-precious stones. From the vestibule (restored), we pass to the Room of Jupiter, named for the fresco of the ceiling. On the walls are splendid *Florentine tapestries* made from cartoons by Stradano (XVI cent.). From here one can reach other, undecorated parts of the Palace and admire the art collection donated to the City of Florence by the American collector Charles Loeser (1928), together with some works which, stolen or mislaid during the last war, have since been recovered. Returning to the Apartment of the Elements, on the left of the fireplace is the entrance to the

**Fig. 11 - Palazzo Vecchio - Sala dell'Udienza (Audience Hall)**

**Room of Cybele.** On the ceiling, the *Triumph of Cybele* and the *Four Seasons.* Against the walls, valuable cabinets (stipi) in tortoise shell and gilded bronze. The floor was made in 1556. From the window observe the third courtyard of the Palace, bordered by the city governement offices. Further ahead is the

**Ceres Room,** that gets its name from the motif on the ceiling, work of Doceno, pupil of Vasari. On the walls are Florentine tapestries with hunting scenes,from cartoons by Stradano. Next is a study-room (that was the vestibule of an old hall) decorated by Vasari who represented *Calliope with Human and Divine Love.* Returning to the stair-case we come to the balcony, built by Cosimo I for the purpose of allowing, his family to watch the parties given in his honor in the Salone dei Cinquecento. Continuing through the corridor we enter the old Quarters of the Priori that Cosimo I had transformed into the *Apartments of his wife Eleanor of Toledo.* The first room is called

**Sala Verde** (Green Room because of the colors of the walls) with grotesque decorations on the ceiling by Ridolfo del Ghirlandaio. On the right is the Chapel frescoed by Bronzino (1564) with *stories of Moses.* By the same artist is the large *Pietà* on the altar. The small closed door on the left wall indicates the beginning of the passage-way that Cosimo I had Vasari build, leading to the Pitti Palace.

**Fig. 12-13 - Palazzo Vecchio - Sala dei Gigli (portal) (Fleur-de-lis Room) - Verrocchio: Winged Boy - Room 16, the former chancellery**

**Room of the Sabines,** from the ceiling decoration. At one time this was the room of the Ladies-in-waiting at the court of Eleonor of Toledo.

**Dining-Room.** On the ceiling, decorated by Stradano, is the *Coronation of Esther* with inscription in honor of Eleonor of Toledo. The room contains a XV cent. lavabo. From the windows observe the view of the courtyard and the first floor where Cosimo I had his apartments, separate from those of his wife, while above, to the right, were their children's apartments, now offices of the city.

**Room of Penelope** (*room II on the plan*). *On the ceiling, Penelope at the loom;* in the frieze, *episodes from the Odyssey.* On the walls: *Madonna and Child,* glazed terracotta and a *Madonna and Child with St. John,* in the manner of Botticelli.

**Private Chamber of Eleanor** called "Room of Gualdrada" from the subject of the ceiling, which Cosimo I had painted alluding to conjugal fidelity and representing the beautiful Gualdrada daughter of Bellincione Berti degli Adimari, who refuses to kiss the Emperor Otto. Against the wall, a cabinet with Florentine mosaic designs. Farther ahead observe the tower incorporated into the Palace. On the cabinet in the corridor is a *Mask of Dante.*

Fig. 14 - Palazzo Vecchio - Sala dei Gigli (Fleur-de-lis Room)

**Chapel of the Signoria.** Dedicated to St. Bernard and containing a *reliquary of the Saint.* The *Annunciation* is by Ridolfo del Ghirlandaio, who frescoed the walls (1514) imitating mosaic. On the altar is a painting representing the *Holy Family* by *Mariano da Pescia.* On the night between the 22-23 of May 1498, Savonarola and his followers spent their last hours in prayer in this chapel.

Following are some rooms, preserved in their original styles.

**Sala delle Udienze** o della Giustizia (fig. 11) (Hall of Justice). Here Savonarola was condemned to death together with his followers Maruffi and Buonvicini. Observe the beautiful carved ceiling, laminated with pure gold, by Benedetto da Maiano and Francione. On the portal of the Chapel, an *inscription in honor of Christ* (1529). The frescoes on the walls, of a highly decorative value representing *Stories of Camillus,* are by the brilliant mannerist artist Francesco Salviati (1550-60). Above the beautiful portal, statue of *Justice* by the brothers Giuliano and Benedetto da Maiano. The doors, inlaid with the figures of *Dante and Petrarch,* are by Giuliano da Maiano and Francione (1481).

**Room of the Lilies** /fig. 14). The magnificent *carved ceiling,* decorated with fleur-de-lys (that we also see on the walls), and the beautiful portal with the *Statue of St. John the Baptist and Putti* (fig. 12) are by Benedetto da Maiano and Francione. On the wall is the ample fresco (restored) by Domenico Ghirlandaio (1481-1485) who represented, from left to right, *Brutus, Muzio Scevola, St. Zanobius between SS. Lorenzo and Stephen, Scipione and Cicero.* From the windows observe the splendid view of the city and the hills of Fiesole. Following on the left is the

**Old Chancellery.** This was Macchiavelli's office when he was Secretary of the Republic. His bust in terracotta and his portraits are by Santi di Tito. In the center of the room, on the pedestal is the famous *Winged Boy* (fig. 13) by Verrocchio, brought here from the courtyard in 1959. Leaving here, on the left is the

**Sala del Guardarobe (Wardrobe),** where the Medici Grand Dukes kept their precious objects. The cupboards and carved ceiling are by Dionigi Nigetti (XVI cent.). On the doors of the cupboards, *53 maps of high scientific* interest, painted by Fra Ignazio Danti (1563) and Don Stefano Buonsignori (1575). In the center of the room the large *"mappa mundi"* ruined by excessive restorations.

In the back of the room, on the right, opening the door inserted between the cupboards, we pass to the terrace from where we can observe the old part of the Palace. Farther ahead.

**The Study,** richly decorated with grotesques. The room was used by Cellini to restore the treasure of the Medici princes. From the little window in the wall, Cosimo I spied his ministers at the meetings of the council held in the Salone dei Cinquecento.

Returning to the small terrace, observe on the left, the *stairs* that the Duke of Athens (driven out in 1343) had built for his security.

Heading toward the exit, returning to the Room of the Lillies, on the left we pass to the landing of the stairs that lead down to some rooms of historical interest, occupied by city offices. Above, the stairs lead to the gallery from where we can enjoy an ample panorama of the city and its hills. If possible, one can climb higher up to the little cell called the "Alberghettino" (little inn) where illustrious prisoners were held, including Cosimo the Elder, before his exile (1344) and Savonarola (1498).

Whoever climbs to the top of the Tower on a beautiful morning cannot forget the panoramic vision afforded from this historic Palace. From here the visitor can admire the city, recognizable in every monument, each of which is associated with a glorious name in history and art. To the north, the vast view of Fiesole and Settignano can be admired. To the south, Piazzale Michelangelo and San Miniato. We can see the Arno that flows slowly toward Pisa, flanked by the green Cascine Park. Farther away, the hills of Chianti. In the background are the Tuscan Apennines and the summits of Vallombrosa. We can observe the function of the Lederle clock and the trap doors that open onto the square below into which, during the defense of the Palace, boiling oil and stones were dropped on the attackers. A bench dropped from here broke the left hand of Michelangelo's David, now restored.

Fig. 15

# THE UFFIZI

Elegant manneristic building (fig. 15), that encloses between two wings the long and narrow Piazzale degli Uffizi, it was built for Cosimo I to house his administrative and judicial offices. It was begun by Giorgio Vasari (1559) and finished in 1585 by Bernardo Buontalenti and Alfonso Parigi. Closed on one side by the Lungarno, the building, with its closely spaced rhythmical and architraved portico, stretches out in ample openings and lengthens the scenary of Signoria Square, joining the Palazzo Vecchio to the Arno. The Uffizi building, last of the post-Michelangelo creations, was inspired by the architecture of the Laurentian Library, although here, the plastic tension of Michelangelo becomes linear and decorative. The sculpture that we see in the niches of the pillars along the portico, representing famous Tuscans, are works of the last century. Among the most notable, that of St. Antonino by Giovanni Dupré (1854), and that of Niccolò Machiavelli by Lorenzo Bartolini (1846).

On the side of the building, facing Via della Ninna, and in the rooms on the ground floor of the Uffizi, can be seen important remains of the Romanesque church of *San Piero Scheraggio,* consecrated in 1608. When the building was constructed, the old church was incorporated into it. The church had been the seat of the community councils; here the popular reforms of Giano della Bella were promulgated (1292); and both Dante and Boccaccio made speeches to the public. The right wing of the Uffizi is preceded by the Mint building, of which only the ground floor remains. Between this building and the beginning of the right wing of the portico, under the arch of Via Lambertesca, opens the Porta delle Suppliche (Door of the Supplications), original architecture of Bernardo Buontalenti, surmounted by a bust of Cosimo I attributed to Giovanni Bandini. Continuing along the Via Lambertesca, to the left can be seen the houses of the Pulci, today seat of the Georgofili, one of the oldest institutions for the study of the economic and agrarian sciences.

The State Archives, until recently housed in the Uffizi Gallery, has now been moved to their new site in Viale Giovine Italia $N^o$ 6. Here we can admire the collection of documents relating to the history of Florence and Tuscany, from their beginning up to modern times. Besides the collections and the specialized library, there is also an interesting exposition in which documents and curious of the history of Florence and Italy can be seen. Among the most famous documents are the Fiorinaio, or register of the Florentine Mint; the charter of union between the Greek and Latin churches (1439); thye book of the Chiodo, containing the condemnation of Dante, and a considerable number of nautical maps.

Under the portico, near the Palazzo Vecchio, between the 19th century statues of *Lorenzo the Magnificent* and *Cosimo the Elder,* is the entrance to the Gallery.

## THE UFFIZI GALLERY
(located on the III floor)

The project to arrange the Gallery on the 3rd floor of this large build-ing, conceived by Cosimo I Medici, was realized by his son Francesco I, who, after having Buontalenti build the room of the Tribune for the col-lection of antique medals and other works of art, had the ceilings of the first corridor decorated so that he could place there the series of fa-mous portraits and, above all, the valuable sculptures, that give it the name of "Gallery of the Sculptures". With the addition of the other rooms, the Gallery was enlarged with the works brought from Rome by Ferdinand I, who renounced the office of Cardinal to become Grand Duke of Tuscany in the place of his deceased brother Francesco I. The Medici (see enclosed genealogical tree), now absolute rulers of the city and of Tuscany, having married into the greatest families, continuously enriched the Gallery, as under the reign of Ferdinando II, who married Vittoria della Rovere. Later Cosimo III had the Gallery made larger in order to house the works inherited from his uncle Cardinal Leopold. With the extinction of the Medici, the last of the family, Anna Maria Ludovica, who died in 1737, with the so called "family-pact" held in Vienna in 1737, arranged that all the art treasures gathered by the pow-erful dynasty forever remain at the disposal of the Florentines and of the visitors of the entire world. Thanks to this testament, it was possible to recuperate so many works of art stolen during the last war, and dur-ing the Napoleonic era, even though, unfortunately, many mas-terpieces remained in France.

The Lorraines, successors of the Medici, enriched the Gallery and built the beautiful room of Niobe to house the marble group called *Niobe*

# PLAN OF THE UFFIZI GALLERY

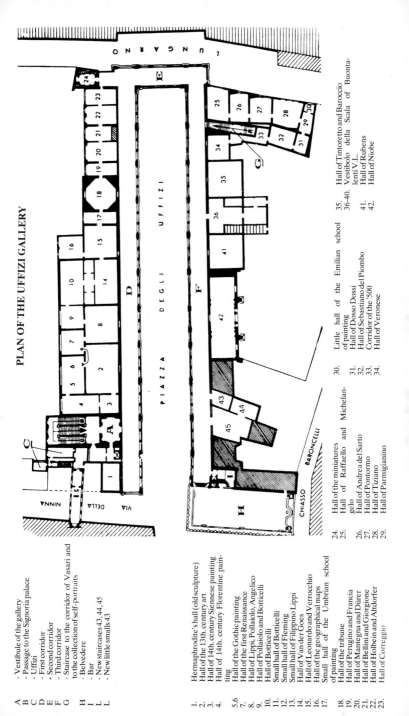

A — Vestibule of the gallery
B — Passage to the Signoria palace
C — Uffizi
D — First corridor
E — Second corridor
F — Third corridor
G — Staircase to the corridor of Vasari and to the collection of self-portraits
H — Belvedere
I — Bar
L — New staircases 43, 44, 45
L — New little smalls 43

1. Hermaphrodite's hall (old sculpture)
2. Hall of the 13th. century art
3. Hall of 14th. century Siennese painting
4. Hall of 14th. century Florentine painting
5.6. Hall of the Gothic painting
7. Hall of the first Renaissance
8. Hall of Lippi, Pollaiolo, Angelico
9. Hall of Pollaiolo and Botticelli
10. Hall of Botticelli
11. Small hall of Botticelli
12. Small hall of Fleming
13. Small hall of Filippino Lippi
14. Hall of Van der Goes
15. Hall of Leonardo and Verrocchio
16. Hall of the geographical maps
17. Small hall of the Umbrian school of painting
18. Hall of the tribune
19. Hall of Perugino and Francia
20. Hall of Mantegna and Durer
21. Hall of Bellini and Giorgione
22. Hall of Holbein and Altdorfer
23. Hall of Correggio

24. Hall of the miniatures
25. Hall of Raffaello and Michelangelo
26. Hall of Andrea del Sarto
27. Hall of Pontormo
28. Hall of Tiziano
29. Hall of Parmigianino
30. Little hall of the Emilian school of painting
31. Hall of Dosso Dossi
32. Hall of Sebastiano del Piombo
33. Corridor of the '500
34. Hall of Veronese
35. Hall of Tintoretto and Baroccio
36-40. Vestibolo della Scala di Buonta- lenti V.L.
41. Hall of Rubens
42. Hall of Niobe

**Fig. 16 - First Corridor of the Gallery**

*and her children* struck by Apollo and Diana. After the expulsionn of the Lorraine (1859), the Gallery passed under the State and was completely reorganized according to modern criteria. With the reorganization that took place after the last war, not only can we more clearly admire the development of Florentine and Tuscan painting and the great influence that it exercised over the other regions, but also we can better observe the great benefits that both Italian and foreign artists obtained by coming into contact with each other, as illustrated by the *Adoration of the Shepherds* by Van der Goes in Room 14, placed in confrontation with works by Florentine artists who were inspired by this painting. Thus the works of Bellini confronted with those of Dürer, clearly show the fascination that the great German artist experienced on contact with the Venetian painters.

**First Vestibule** with the ticket counter, where an antique copy of the marble group of *Mars and Venus* has been placed. Of recent date is the reorganization of the presbytery and the apse of San Piero Scheraggio, that contains frescoes detached from various Florentine churches.

**Second Vestibule.** On the left wall dominates the large portrait of the Flemish school representing *Anna Maria Ludovica de' Medici*. On the

**Figs. 17-18 - Giotto and Cimabue: Madonna Enthroned with Angels**

right wall, columns of the old church of San Piero Scheraggio, on which remains of 13th century frescoes can be detected. On the left begins the monumental staircase by Vasari, decorated with ancient Roman busts.

On the first floor is located the famous collection of *Drawings and Prints* begun by Cardinal Leopold de' Medici, reserved for scholars. In the first room periodically are held expositions of graphics and drawings by foreign and Italian artists, to which no entrance fee is charged.

In order to avoid the 126 step climb of the staircase, it is advisable to use the lift that takes you to the top floor. Before entering the Gallery, one can admire Vasari's splendid staircase. Past the ticket control is the vestibule decorated with panoplies and trophies of late Roman art.

**First corridor of the Gallery** (fig. 16). From the windows observe the architectonic complex of the building, erected by the Medici to house their administrative offices on the first floor. The long loggia that originally topped the building was closed with wide windows.

The frescoes of the ceiling in this first corridor, with mythological and grotesque motives, were painted by the Florentine artists Bizzelli, Butteri, Pieroni and Alessandro Allori in 1581, inspired by the Vatican Loggia. Badly damaged on the night of August 4, 1944, when the Germans blew up the bridges over the Arno, these valuable frescoes, that

Fig. 19

because of so many catastrophies seemed irreparably lost, were able to be restored after four years of patient and able restoration. On the wall of the long corridor is the rich series of Belgian tapestries representing scenes of *Festivities and Tournaments at the Court of Catherine de' Medici and Henry III,,* the cartoons of which are attributed to François Quesnell (1575-80).

The visit to the Gallery begins in

**Room 2,** *dedicated to Cimabue and Giotto.* In direct confrontation Giotto and Cimabue: Madonnas Enthroned with Angels. Also other artists of the same period. On the right wall we see the famous *Madonna enthroned with Angels* by Cimabue (fig. 18), originally in the church of St. Trinità, dated around 1275. A work greatly nourished by the Byzantine culture, especially in the soft colors, in the gold touches of the Madonna's dress and in the details of the drawing, obtained in the perspective of the throne and the degrading of the angels that reveals, with the beginning of a new style, the foundations of the future evolution of Florentine art.

On the left wall, opposite to Cimabue, the famous *Madonna and Child with Angels* formerly in the Rucellai Chapel in Santa Maria Novella, for centuries believed to be by Cimabue, is attributed to Duccio di Buoninsegna, although authoritative critics still believe it to be the work of a master between Cimabue and Duccio, known as the "Master of the Rucellai Madonna". The solemnty of the painting, with its traditionally Byzantine colors, with the majestic figure of the Madonna and the Prophets and Saints in the beautiful frame rendered with a miniaturist's delicacy, contribute to assigning this work to Duccio.

In front of the entrance dominates the famous, grandiose *Madonna Enthroned with Angels and Saints* by Giotto (fig. 17), originally in the church of Ognissanti. One of the most solemn creations of this great innovator of Florentine and Italian art, chronologically placed between the frescoes of Assisi and those in the Scrovegni Chapel in Padua (1303-05). In this work Giotto discloses all his powerful personality as far as space and form are concerned. While the color contributes for the first time in illuminating the figures, rendered profoundly human, the soft chiaroscuro helps to make this great work compact, volumetric and monumental.

Also by Giotto is the *Polyptych* displayed on the left, that came from the Church of the Badia.

On the wall beginning left of the entrance are: *Madonna and Child* (Florentine school, c. 1270); *Crucifix and Stories of the Passion* (Lucchese school, middle of the 13th cent.); *St. Luke* by the "Master of

Fig. 20 - Gentile da Fabriano: Adoration of the Magi

Fig. 21 - Paolo Uccello: Battle of San Romano

the Maddalena". On the right wall from the entrance are: the *Stigmata of St. Francis and Christ Crucified,* in the manner of Bonaventura Berlinghieri; the *Savior between the Virgin and SS. Peter, John and Paul* by Meliore Toscano (c. 1271). On the following wall, *Crucifix and Stories of the Passion,* Pisan school of the middle of the 12th century.
Then follows

**Room 3,** *dedicated to 14th century Sienese painting.* Beginning on the left, *Stories of the Life of the Beata Umiltà,* originally in the church of the Donne di Faenza; followed by a *Nativity* by the Bolognese painter Simone de' Crocifissi, and a *Presentation in the Temple* by the Sienese Bonaccorsi. Then the famous *Annunciation* by Simone Martini (1333), originally in the Cathedral of Siena, one of the most important creations by this leader of the Sienese school, rendered with musical rhythm and a miniaturistic quality (fig. 19). On the sides observe the figures of *SS. Ansanus and Giuditta* by Lippo Memmi, pupil and brother-in-law of Simone, who attempts to emulate the fluidity of line and delicate form of the master. The room also contains the *Madonna and Child* by the Sienese Niccolò di Ser Sozzo Tegliacci (the date can be read 1315 or 1341), and, the *Four Stories of the Life of St. Nicola di Bari* and the delicate *Presentation in the Temple* (the latter dated 1342) by Ambrogio Lorenzetti, brother of Piero, and with him considered one of the most important Sienese artists of the 14th century.

**Room 4.** *Dedicated to 14th century Florentine painting. On the long left wall are shown fragments of a polyptych with Saints, Martyrs and Virgins,* by the Lombard Giovanni da Milano, of northern formation, which he reveals in the soft chiaroscuro rendered with acute realism, but at the same time, aware of the art of Giotto. This is followed by the grandiose painting by Andrea Orcagna, representing St. Matthew. On the following wall, *Madonna and Saints,* polyptych of Bernardo Daddi. On the right wall, *Deposition,* attributed to Giottino, once thought to be by Maso di Banco, very close (perhaps the greatest) follower of Giotto. Giottino is one of the most remarkable Florentine painters of the 14th century, sensitive to northern color and to soft chiaroscuro. Next, *Madonna and Child with Angels* by the Florentine artist Taddeo Gaddi, one of the most faithful followers of Giotto. Also shown are works by Nardo di Cione, Bernardo Daddi, Jacopo del Casentino and others.

**Rooms 5-6.** *Dedicated to works by artists of the so called "International Gothic" that flourished between the end of the 14th century and the beginning of the 15th century.* From left entering, the famous *Adoration of the Magi,* by Lorenzo Monaco, teacher of Beato Angelico (circa 1420), bright and fantastic work by this Sienese artist who was active in Flor-

**Fig. 22 -Masaccio and Masolino: St. Anne Enthroned with the Madonna and Child**
**Fig. 23 - Piero della Francesca: Portrait of Battista Sforza**
**Fig. 24 - Piero della Francesca: Portrait of Federico da Montefeltro**

ence and became one of the major late Gothic painters.

On the wall in front is the *Adoration of the Magi* by Gentile da Fabriano (fig. 20), formerly in the church of St. Trinità. Gentile is a late Gothic artist, fantastic and courtly, while his deep color and plastic values are already Renaissance. On the following wall, by the same artist: *Four Saints,* fragment of a work once in the Quaratesi Chapel in San Niccolò, dated about 1424. Next the large *Incoronation of the Virgin* by Lorenzo Monaco (1413). On the small back wall, the graceful and imaginative *Tebaide,* representing the life of the hermits in the desert, believed by some critics to be by Gherardo Starnina, and by others, by the hand of Beato Angelico, during the period when Masaccio's influence was greatly felt.

**Room 7.** *Dedicated to early Renaissance.* On the left wall the famous *Battle of San Romano* by Paolo Uccello (1456) (fig. 21). It is the central part of a series of paintings, one of which is in the Louvre, and the other in the National Gallery of London. The artist, in his tense perspective study, here faces the typical Renaissance problems of foreshortenings, crystallizing figures, landscapes, horses, armor and arms in immobile volumes.

On the easel, the famous *Portraits of Federico da Montefeltro Duke of Urbino and his Wife Battista Sforza* (figs 23-24) by Piero della Francesca (1456-66). On the back, the *Triumphs of the Duke and Duchess.* He represents the subjects on marble terraces against a midday sun that hits the distant landscape. A creation rendered with an extremely poetic geometric abstraction, exalted in the fullness of the light, against a vast landscape. Here the Flemish suggestions are surpassed in a completely new synthetic vision. With the inheritance of Vittoria della Rovere, wife of Ferdinand II Medici, the work passed over to the Uffizi in 1631, together with other art treasures.

On the opposite wall, *St. Anne Enthroned with the Madonna and Child* (fig. 22), work done in collaboration by Masolino and Masaccio, who shows a style already full and mature, despite his young age. On the right, *Madonna Enthroned with Saints* (c. 1445), by Domenico Veneziano, formerly in the church of St. Lucia de' Magnoli, a work which vibrates with the color rendered luminous by the daylight that covers the spaces and palpitates in the figures painted with intense humanity. On the next wall, *Madonna and Child,* by Beato Angelico, *Coronation of the Virgin,* also by Beato Angelico, (Fig. 25) which can be admired in all its magnificence only in Florence in the Convent of St. Mark. In both these works Beato Angelico succeeded in uniting miniaturistic detail with the monumentality of the composition, already in full Renaissance style.

Fig. 25 - Beato Angelico: Incoronation of the Virgin

**Room 8.** *Dedicated to Filippo Lippi.* Here we can admire the famous *Madonna and Child with Two Angels* (fig. 26) by Filippo Lippi, whose art was formed under the influence of Masaccio, especially in the plastic construction of the figures.

On the easel: *Madonna of the Rose Garden* by Sandro Botticelli, whose works can be seen better in the following rooms: The painter was still under the influence of the Master Filippo Lippi at that time. Above the door to the corridor is the *Resurrection of Lazarus* by the Flemish painter Nicolas Froment who died at Avignon.

On the far wall, large *Incoronation of the Virgin,* early work of Filippo Lippi. Finally, on the next wall, to the left, *Madonna and Child* and *Annunciation* by Alessio Baldovinetti, pupil of Domenico Veneziano, more sensitive toward linearity than light values.

**Room 9.** *Dedicated to the Pollaiolo brothers* . On entering to the right, *Three Virtues* by Piero del Pollaiolo: on the back of the first one observe the vigorous sketch of *Charity,* by his brother Antonio, a great gold smith and sculptor of the second half of the 15th century. By Antonio are the other three *Virtues* on the next wall, beside the *Fortitude* by Botticelli, executed for the stalls of the Merchant's Tribunal. Comparing these works permits us to observe how these two artists, with their common vibrating lines, arrived at different results.

Some particularly precious works can be admired in the showcase between the windows. Biblical subjects by Botticelli, *Judith with her Handmaid carrying the head of Holofernes,* and *Holofernes Slain in his Tent;* by Antonio del Pollaiolo, *Hercules and the Hydra* and *Hercules and Antaeus,* small replicas by the artist himself, of the large canvases painted for the Medici Palace. Also by Antonio, the *Portrait of a Gentlewoman* and the portrait of *Galeazzo Maria Sforza* which came from the room of Lorenzo the Magnificent. On the left, the *Saints Vincent, James and Eustace,* an altar-piece from the Basilica of San Miniato, by the brothers Piero and Antonio, principally by Antonio who was the elder.

**Rooms 10 to 14.** Dedicated to the latter half of the XV Century and to Sandro Botticelli. From left to right as far as the door: the most significant collection of the works of Sandro Botticelli, typical representative of the humanistic Florence of Lorenzo the Magnificent and of Poliziano. Filippino Lippi painted the delicate *Selfportrait* (Fig. 32) and the incisive *Portrait of an Old Florentine.* Between the luminous and musical *Madonna of the Magnificat* and the melancholy *Madonna of the Pomegranate,* both of around 1480, one can admire the celebrated *Birth of Venus* (Fig. 31), which the artist painted on canvas (1486), idealising the beautiful and fragile Simonetta, beloved of Giuliano the brother of Lorenzo the Magnificent.

This is a rhythmic creation with delicate colouring rendered with the cold tones of a marine dawn, inspired by Poliziano's verses. On the right, the *Minerva with the Centaur,* a subject of classical inspiration, an allegorical representation of "knowledge which dominates strength".

The following works in small format include the well-known *Calumny,* which Botticelli is said to have painted when incited by Savonarola's sermons. The scene is represented under the static architecture of a beautiful classical portico, with in the background a stretch of open sea beneath a serene sky. The compact group of figures lends a vigorous animation to the scene (Fig. 31) in which even the statues in the niches seem to partecipate. In this drama alluding to human injustice King Midas, with ass' ears, sits on the throne listening to the very worst of

Fig. 26

Fig. 27 - Botticelli: Portrait of an Unknown Man
Fig. 28 - A. Pollaiolo: Portrait of a Noblewoman
Fig. 29 - Botticelli: Allegory of Springtime

Fig. 30-31 - Botticelli: Allegory of the Birth of Venus, and Calumny

counsellors, Ignorance and Suspicion. The hooded man is Calumny who raises his hand towards the foolish King to add solemnity to what he is about to say. Envy, Deceit and Hypocrisy are the three women dragging the Innocent victim before the King. On the left is Remorse under the sembiance of an old man, hooded, dazzled by the sight of the naked Truth who gazes serenely towards Heaven. Next, one can admire the *Allegory of Spring* (Fig. 29). The lyrical scene which is set in the fresh green forest, is dominated by the bright clothed figure of Venus genitrix.

On the right are the figures of Spring strewing flowers and Flora followed by Zephyr. On the left, the famous Three Graces who, seen through their transparent veils, begin to dance while being shot at with arrows by the blindfolded Cupid, and the figure of Mercury clearing away the last of the morning mist.

On the left of the door, the *Adoration of the Magi* (1475), where three generations of the House of the Medici can be seen, idealised, among the personages: Cosimo the Elder at the top, at the bottom the two sons Piero and Giovanni; lower down on the left, Lorenzo the Magnificent leaning on his sword (representing power); on the right dark-haired Giuliano who loved the lovely Simonetta. The figure in the yellow robe is believed to be a selfportrait of Botticelli.

On the easel beyond the door, *St. Jerome,* the work of Botticelli's principal pupil, Filippino Lippi, son of Fra' Filippo. This part of the room is dominated by the great *Portinari Triptych* by Van der Goes. Painted in Bruges (1476-78) for Thomas Portinari, representative in that city of the Medici Bank.

In the central panel *Adoration of the Shepherds* (Fig. 33); on the left panel St. Anthony and St. Thomas, with the commissioner himself and his two sons; on the right panel, St. Margherita and St. Mary Magdalen with Maria Portinari and her daughter. This work is justly famous for the subtle and poetic human observation of the figures and of Nature, rendered with subtle and complex shading of colour. Splendid figures in chiaroscuro representing the Annunciation are painted on the rear panels of the left and right leaves of the triptych, which were normally kept closed to protect the central painting. Behind the triptych is the *Deposition* by Rogier Van der Weyden, painted, it is believed, during his stay in Italy.

Displayed on the surrounding walls, on the other hand, are works by Lorenzo di Credi, (Venus), Ghirlandaio *(Adoration of the Magi* and the predella with *Stories of Saints)* , and again Filippini Lippi, the *Altarpiece of the Eight* and the *Adoration of the Magi*; Florentine artists who

Fig. 32 - Filippino Lippi: Self-portrait

Fig. 33

**Fig. 34 - Lorenzo di Credi: Annunciation**

in various ways, and to different extent felt the fascination of Flemish painting. Continuing the tour of this room we find other Botticelli works, the grandiose *Altarpiece of St. Barnabas* and the small panel representing *St. Bernardino in the Study*. Near the door, the enigmatic *Portrait of a Young Man* with a medal of Cosimo the Elder, perhaps the artist's brother.

**Room 15.** *Verrocchio, Signorelli, Leonardo and others of their group.* On the left, is the *Annunciation* (fig. 34) by Lorenzo di Credi, sensitive to the influence of his fellow apprentice Leonardo. The painting, of modest proportions, is the most valuable work of the artist, who, in the school of Verrocchio, surpassed the pictorial quality of the master.

At the either side of the entrance, two monumental *Altarpieces* by Signorelli, an artist formed in the Umbrian figurative school but attentive to the teachings of the Florentines. Another Umbrian and very famous at the time, is Perugino (Pietro Vannucchi), whose melancholy temperament can be appreciated in his distressful *Pietà*. Next the famous painting of the *Baptism of Christ* (fig. 35), that Verrocchio, more well known as a sculptor than as a painter, began in 1470 with the help of the young Leonardo, whose hand is recognized in the angel to the left shown in profile. A simple and luminous painting, with a suggestively beautiful landscape.

The central wall is dominated by the celebrated *Adoration of the Magi*

**Fig. 35: Verrocchio: Baptism of Christ**

by Leonardo da Vinci (fig. 36), painted for the brothers of the church of San Donato Scopeto, left incomplete by the great artist and scientist who was called to Milan by Ludovico il Moro. Despite the fact that the painting is left in its preparatory state, we can see the importance of Leonardo's invention of «sfumato» (shading), that was so widely diffused in the successive Lombard and Tuscan schools of painting. Also notice the solemnity of the scene, shown in a pyramid composition, the majesty of the architectonic and landscape elements, and the extraordinary variety of human types and expressions. This work reveals

**Fig. 36 - Leonardo: Adoration of the Magi**

Leonardo's personality in full, his continuous and tireless research and attention to nature and humanity in all its aspects. In addition this room contains the famous and much discussed Annunciation (Fig. 37), with the luminous and idealized Tuscan landscape, which Leonardo is believed to have painted in Verrocchio's workshop.

**Room 16.** *Called of the Maps,* because maps of Tuscany were painted on the walls by Stefano Buonsignori (1589). Continuing along the corridor, we arrive at Room 18, the Tribune. From here, through a small door on the left we enter:

**Room 17.** Where, after the recent restorations, the statue of the *Hermaphrodite,* (formerly in room 1), has been placed. According to the original disposition of the room, the small niches in the wall have been brought back to light, and bronze and marble statuettes placed in them. We return from this room to

**Room 18.** «*Tribune*», built by Buontalenti (1585-89), and decorated with shells by Pocchetti. In the center, the famous *Medici Venus,* Roman copy of an original Hellenistic work of the end of the 4th century B.C., found in Hadrian's Villa in Rome. The other statues, also Roman copies of Greek exemplaries, represent: the *Knife Whetter,* the *Wrestlers,* and the *Dancing Faun.* In the niche of the Tribune is a cabinet of ebony with inlaid Florentine mosaic. On the walls are splendid portraits of the Medici; among the most important, *Cosimo the Elder* by Pontormo (fig.38); *Lorenzo the Magnificent,* by Vasari (fig.39); *Lucrezia* (fig. 40) *and Bartolomeo Panciatichi,* by Bronzino, a refined portrait painter who also painted the portraits of *Cosimo I* and his wife *Eleanor of Toledo,* shown with her son *Giovanni;* by the same artist are the gr-

Fig. 37 - Leonardo: Annunciation

acious children of Cosimo and Eleanor, don Garcia (fig. 41) and Isabella (fig. 42). Also of note in this room is the charming *Musical Angel* by Rosso Fiorentino.

**Room 19.** *Dedicated to Perugino and Signorelli.* By Perugino we notice the two *Portraits of Vallombrosian Monks,* with warm chiaroscuro and intense spirituality; the famous *Young Man,* believed to be Alessandro Braccesi (fig. 43). Of the Cortona painter Signorelli, we have the representative work, the large *Holy Family.* He is one of the most interesting artists of the second half of the XV Century. Sensitive to the spatial teachings of Piero della Francesca, he was inspired by the shading of Leonardo and the drawing of Pollaiolo, which gave his creations both volume and movement.

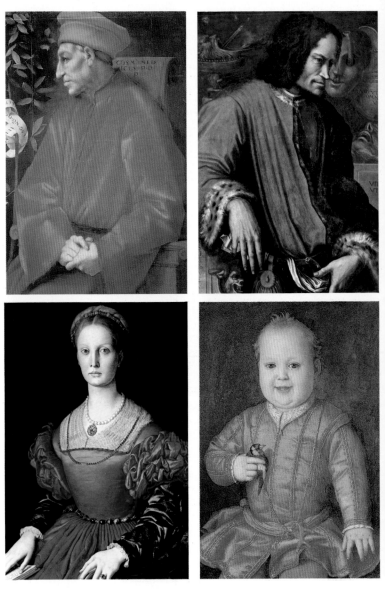

Fig. 38 - Pontormo: Portrait of Cosimo the Elder
Fig. 39 - Vasari: Lorenzo the Magnificent
Fig. 40 - Bronzino: Portrait of Lucrezia Panciatichi
Fig. 41 - Bronzino: Portrait of the Medici Prince don Garcia

Fig. 42 - Bronzino: Portrait of Princess  Isabella Medici
Fig. 43 - Perugino: Portrait of Young Man
Fig. 44 - Mantegna: Triptych of the "Madonna of the Caves"

Observe the *Portrait of Evangelista Scappi* by Francesco Francia, pupil of Perugino; and by Lorenzo Costa, the *Portrait of Giovanni II Bentivoglio* and the small *St. Sebastian.* Here also can be seen two fragmentary paintings by Melozzo da Forlì showing the *Annunciation,* that was repainted on the back of *St. Benedict* and *St. John the Baptist.*

**Room 20.** *Dürer and the German painters.* Here are shown *Adam* and *Eve* by Lukas Cranach, influenced by Dürer. On the right, by Cranach, *Portrait of Martin Luther and his wife Catherine Bore* and the large *self-portrait.* On the followings walls, portraits of *Luther,* of *Melantone,* and *Johann I* and *Friedrich II,* Electors of Saxony, also by Cranach, and the Portrait of *Ferdinand of Castille* by Hans Maler (16th century). By the great German painter and engraver Albrecht Dürer, who sojourned in Italy for a long time and felt the charm of the Venetians, we can admire a *Madonna and Child,* the *Portrait of his Father* (1490) and the celebrated *Adoration of the Magi* (1504 - fig. 45). Evidence of his contact with Bellini (see following room) in the Republic of St. Mark, can be seen in his *St. Philip Apostle and St. James Major,* both fundamental for the completion of the range of his mature works.
Observe also the *St. Domenic* by the imaginative master and head of the Ferrarese school Cosmè Tura, and the 15th century copy of Dürer's *Adam and Eve,* conserved in the Prado of Madrid. On the wall, panels with *Stories of SS. Peter and Paul.* Also, a *landscape* by Hans Brueghel, on the back of which is a *Calvary* taken from Dürer's engravings. On the ceiling, notice the Signoria, St. Maria Novella, and St. Croce Squares (St. Croce church without its present façade).

**Room 21.** *Dedicated to Giovanni Bellini, to his pupil Giorgione and others of their school.* Here we can admire the famous *Allegory of Purgatory* (fig. 46) by Giovanni Bellini, inspired by a 13th century French poem, and a dramatic *Pietà* (datable circa 1490). Although in this work, color, the fundamental element of Bellini's painting, is absent, we can still observe the tonal sensitivity of his art, through the luminous and silvery rendering of the «grisaille». Cima da Conegliano, follower of Bellini, is present here with a *Madonna and Child,* with light and transparent colors. By Giorgione we admire the *Judgement of Solomon* and *Moses as a Child before the Pharoah,* extremely delicate works, rendered with an acute spirit of observation for the landscape (fig. 47). On the wall, tapestry of the *Deposition* executed by Nicholas Karcher (1549-1553), from a cartoon by Francesco Salviati. In the following room are other tapestries by the same authors, representing the *Ascension* and

*Ecce Homo.* Observe on the wall above the tapestry, the war ruins around the Ponte Vecchio (1944), frescoed by the restorers after the liberation of the city.

**Room 22.** *Dedicated to the works of Flemish and German painters.* Together with the delicate works by the Flemish master Gerard David, are displayed paintings by the German artist Altdorfer, such as the *Departure* and the *Martyrdom of St. Florian*; followed by the portrait of *Sir Richard Southwell*, by Hans Holbein the Younger, painted during his sojourn in England. Present are works by other Flemish and Dutch masters of the early 16th century.

**Room 23.** *Dedicated to Antonio Allegri called il Correggio*, an artist who unites echoes of Mantegna to a remarkable sensitivity to Leonardo's «sfumato» (shading). Among his works shown in this room we remember the famous *Virgin adoring the Child* (fig. 48). On the opposite wall, works by Flemish painters Bernaert van Orley, Quentin Massys, and Joos van Cleve. On the successive walls, paintings by Leonardo's followers, among whom, Luini, Antonio Bazzi called il Sodoma, and an old copy of *Madonna and Child,* from an original by Leonardo, preserved at the Louvre.
By Andrea Mantegna, among the most representative painters in the artistic ambient of Northern Italy, is the small but grandly conceived *Madonna of the Caves.*

**Room 24.** Room of the Miniatures (generally closed). The room, delicately decorated in the 17th century, was destined for the safekeeping of jewels, that are now kept in the Pitti Palace. The room contains the valuable collection of miniatures on ivory and parchment by Italian and foreign artists. Notice the miniature of *Paolina Buonaparte,* Borghese Princess and Napoleon's sister, by the Swiss artist Counis, whose self-portrait is also shown.

**Second Corridor**, joining the two wings of the Uffizi. Observe the beautiful ceiling decorated in the 16th century. In the corridor are various classical sculptures, among which the *Boy taking a Thorn from his Foot;* a sarcophagus with a scene showing the *Fall of Phaeton,* Roman art of the II century; and the graceful *Girl Seated in the Act of Preparing to Dance*, Hellenistic copy (3rd century B.C.). From the central windows, a splendid view of Signoria Square, Palazzo Vecchio and the Duomo. From the lateral windows, view of the southern side of the city, with the hills of Bellosguardo, the bridges over the Arno (fig. 49), and

Fig. 45

**Fig. 46 - Bellini: Allegory of Purgatory**

the Vasarian corridor that, passing over the top of the Ponte Vecchio, reaches the Pitti Palace on the Boboli hillside to the left.

**Third Corridor.** Among the numerous classical statues and interesting Roman busts of the 3rd and 4th centuries, we notice at the beginning of the corridor, two statues representing *Marsyas Hanging,* Roman copies of original Greek works. On the walls, three series of tapestries: first, of Florentine manufacture, from cartoons by Allori and Cigoli, showing *Scenes of the Passion of Christ*; the other two were made in Brussels and represent *Stories of Jacob* and *Battle scenes.* The beautiful ceiling, decorated with historical and mythological subjects by 17th century painters, was damaged during the last war like the other, and has been restored. After Room 25, the glass door opens on to the Vasarian Corridor (1564) that, after being damaged in 1944 and during the flood of 1966, has been largely restored. In the first section of this long corridor, a great part of the collection of self-portraits by Italian and foreign artists are displayed. To name a few are those of Titian, Andrea del Sarto, Vasari, Rubens, David, Ingres, Corot, Mancini, Canova etc. Raphael's self-portrait is shown in Room 25 together with his works.

**Room 25.** *Dedicated to Michelangelo and to the Florentines*. Opposite the entrance we can admire the celebrated roundel in which is painted

Fig. 47 - Giorgione: Moses as a Child
Fig. 48 - Correggio: Adoration of the Child
Fig. 49 - View of the Ponte Vecchio and the other bridges from the second Corridor of the Uffizi Gallery

the *Holy Family* by Michelangelo (Fig. 53) painted for the marriage of Agnolo Doni to Maddalena Strozzi between 1504 and 1505. This is a rare and prestigious work, in spiral form, where, in a barely suggested landscape, the titanic artist represented powerful, athletic figures of plastic nudes foreshadowing the frescoes of the Sistine Chapel. The work is rendered powerfully dramatic by the figures in the foreground. The splendid frame with the arms of the Doni family was carried out by the carver Domenico del Tasso to a design, it would seem, by Michelangelo.

With this fundamental work Michelangelo became the initiator of a "manner" which was to last for an entire century. The room contains works by Rosso Fiorentino and other artists, called "mannerists", because they were followers of the "manner" of the great masters, Michelangelo in particular. There are also displayed the works of the Spaniard Berruguete, who was in Italy to study the brillant Florentine painters in this style.

Next to the entrance is the famous *Visitation* by Albertinelli (1503, Fig. 54) exhibited here with other selected works executed possibly in the period in which he was the friend and collaborator of Fra' Bartolomeo. A large, solemn work rendered with profound humanity, which influenced Raphael's work during his Florentine period. In the same room: *Joseph presenting his Father and Brothers to the Pharoah*, by Granacci; a portrait of Perugino attributed to Raphael, his pupil. Another work by a "mannerist" Rosso Fiorentino, very close to Michelangelo, is the painting on board *Moses defends the Daughters of Jetrus*, with acute dramatic sense and vigorous emphasis.

**Room 26.** Raphael and Andrea del Sarto. (Andrea d'Agnolo after his father's profession of sarto or tailor). The works shown here, along with those in the preceding room, give a clear picture of the art of the two great masters of the high Renaissance. Dominating the work of Raphael Sanzio, who sums up all the pictorial problematics of his time and opens new solutions to painting, is the celebrated *Portrait of Pope Leo X* (1519, Fig. 52) seated between Cardinal Julius, his cousin, later Pope Clement VII, the two Popes of the Medici family) on the left, and on the right Luigi de' Rossi, Secretary to them both. On the left, near the window, the *Portrait of Francis Maria della Rovere* a youthful work; followed by a self-portrait of the artist (Fig. 50) and the *Madonna of the Goldfinch*, with a fine Umbrian landscape, a work of his Florentine period. On the right there follows a *Portrait of Pope Julius II della Rovere*, a splendid old copy.

Fig. 50 - Raphael: Self-portrait
Fig. 51 - Raphael: Madonna of the Goldfinch
Fig. 52 - Raphael: Leo X among the Cardinals
Fig. 53 - Michelangelo: Holy Family

Here, among other works, we have the well known *Madonna of the Harpies* (1517, Fig. 55) by Andrea del Sarto, which has been named thus for the small harpies which form the decoration of the pedestal on which the Madonna stands. A softly chiaro-scuro composition with harmoniously arranged figures.

**Room 27.** *Pontormo.* Jacopo Carrucci, born in Pontormo near Empoli (1494), a contemporary of Piero di Cosimo and Andrea del Sarto. He was influenced by Michelangelo and by Dürer's engravings, and became a mediate artist, creator of tormented and restless works, as shown here in his celebrated *Supper at Emmàus* (fig. 56). Among the other works in the room notice the predellą with *Stories of St. Acacius*, by the Florentine Francesco Ubertini called il Bachiacca, genial designer of cartoons for tapestries. The Sienese painter Beccafumi is duly represented with some of his works.

**Room 28.** *Dedicated to Titian*, the greatest Venetian artist of the 16th century, who brought the luminous tonality of Giovanni Bellini and Giorgione to the supreme height of color but was, at the same time, sensitive to Florentine and Roman expression. Beginning from the right wall we have: *Portrait of Catherine Cornaro,* with the attributes of St. Catherine of Alexandria (old copy of a lost original). Following: *Flora,* live and passionate woman, rendered with intense color; *Venus of Urbino* (fig. 57), painted in 1538 for the Duke of Urbino, Ubaldo II della Rovere. This famous reclining Venus, with its vibrant color, is shown in a rich environment, made more realistic by the figures of the hand-maids looking for clothes. The light that penetrates from the window, limits the landscape and illuminates the room. Next, a *Knight of Malta,* at one time attributed to Giorgione, but now considered one of Titian's masterpieces, from the period when he was under the master's influence. By Palma il Vecchio, follower of Titian, we see the exuberant *Judith.* On the following walls: Portraits of *Francesco Maria della Rovere* and *Eleonora Gonzaga della Rovere,* Dukes of Urbino, by Titian. On the last wall the shapely *Venus and Cupid,* that Titian painted at the age of 73 years with the help of his pupils.

**Room 29.** *Parmigianino* (Francesco Mazzola da Parma 1503-1540). Refined painter of the Correggesque current who, aware of the Florentine and Roman styles, became the most original mannerist artist, as can be seen by his graceful *Madonna* called «*Of the Long Neck*» (fig. 58). The room also contains works by Dosso Dossi and Lucrezia Fontana from Bologna.

Fig. 54

Fig. 55 - A. Del Sarto: Madonna of the Harpies

Fig. 56

**Room 30.** *Dedicated to Dossi,* together with other artists of his group, thus completing the panorama of Emilian painting.

**Room 31.** Contains a few works by Dossi and other Emilian and Venetian painters. From the window, a marvelous view of the Palazzo Vecchio, the Duomo and the nearby church of Orsanmichele on the left.

**Room 32.** *Sebastiano del Piombo and other Venetian artists.* On the central wall: the *Death of Adonis,* with a panorama of 16th century Venice in the background (fig. 59). Works of Sebastiano del Piombo, a Venetian of Giorgionesque formation, but active in Rome, who was aware of the coloristic suggestions of Raphael and the plastic values of Michelangelo. On the next wall, *Sacred Conversation* by Lorenzo Lotto.

**Room 33.** Consists of a small corridor where we see a graceful antique Bacchus in the corner. Among the other works here are a *Self-portrait* by Antonio Moro (Flemish); *Christ bearing the Cross* by Morales (Spanish); and a *Portrait of Francis I King of France* by Clouet (French). Then, in the corridor itself, a *Medusa,* Flemish school of the 16th century, and small works by Florentine and Tuscan mannerists, among whom Ligozzi, Vasari, Allori, Zucchi and numerous other artists from this period. Finally, observe on the small back wall, the *Three Graces* by Poppi.

**Room 34.** *Paolo Veronese.* An artist expecially famous for the luminous and realistic rendering of the drapery. Among his works, the *Holy Family with St. Barbara* (fig. 60). The room contains two paintings by the great portrait painter G. Battista Moroni of Bergamo; *Portraits* by Campi of Cremona, the *Transfiguration* by Girolamo Savoldo of Brescia, and works of their period.

**Room 35.** *Dedicated to Tintoretto* (Jacopo Robusti, 1519-94), Baroccio (Federico Fiori, 1528-1612) from Urbino, and Jacopo Bassano (c. 1515-92). With Tintoretto and Bassano, Venetian color arrives at true luministic painting as appears in *Leda and the Swan* (fig. 61) by Tintoretto. He is also great as a portrait painter, as is proven by the *Portrait of Jacopo Sansovino* shown here on the right. The formal elegance and the luminous research of Bassano are best realized in nocturnal and genre scenes, as shown in the *Roveto ardente* on the back wall. By Baroccio, artist of a complex formation, we can admire the grandiose *Ma-*

Fig. 57

**Fig. 58 - Parmigianino: Madonna of the Long Neck**

Fig. 59 - Sebastiano del Piombo: Death of Adonis
Fig. 60 - Veronese: Holy Family with S. Barbara

**Fig. 61 - Tintoretto: Leda and the Swan**

*donna del Popolo.* The room also contains works by Leandro Bassano, lesser known follower of his father Jacopo, by the modest Domenico, son of the great Tintoretto, and by Palma the Younger, who continues Titian's heredity with that coloristic exuberance that identifies the early 17th century.

The staircase of Buontalenti gives access to a beautiful *Vestibule,* where are displayed a marble *wildboar,* a bronze copy of which was made by Pietro Tacca for the fountain in the Straw Market, and the *Torso of a Satyr,* Greek art of the 2nd century A.D. Also shown are elegant Medicean tapestries. The narrow staircase leads to the Loggia of the Uffizi, therefore it is used as an exit.

**Room 41.** *Dedicated to Rubens* (1577-1640). Heroic and passionate personality, formed in Rome and Venice, he reaches the height of expression on his return to Antwerp (1608). We can admire his large canvases of *Henry IV at the Battle of Ivry, Triumphant Entry of Henry IV into Paris,* and the small *Portrait of his wife Isabella Brandt* (fig. 62), a work of pleasant and poetic intimacy. Of Rubens' school notice the *Portrait of Galileo Galilei* (fig. 63), by Sustermans, Flemish painter active at the

Fig. 62 - Rubens: Portrait of Isabella Brandt
Fig. 63 - Sustermans: Portrait of G. Galilei
Fig. 64 - Canaletto: View of Venice

Medici court; *Portrait of Giovanni di Montfort,* by Van Dyck, and, by the Genoese Gaulli called il Baciccio, the *portrait of Cardinal Leopold de' Medici.*

**Room 42.** *Room of Niobe.* This room was made by Grand Duke Pietro Leopold of Lorraine, who commissioned the architect Gasparre M. Paoletti to build it (1777-80) to hold the group of *Niobe and her Children,* Roman copy an original Hellenistic work of the III-II cent. B.C. The style of the architecture is neo-classic. The group of statues was found in Rome in 1583. In the center is a *marble vase* of the 3rd century belonging to the Medici collection. The walls of this splendid room are enriched by Medicean tapestries representing *episodes from the Lives of the Medici Grand Dukes,* and, on the opposite wall, *Stories of Moses.*

**Room 43.** *Caravaggio.* Here we can admire the *Medusa* (Fig. 66) of this great innovator of Italian painting (Michelangelo Merisi from Caravaggio near Bergamo, 1573 - 1610), who exercised enormous influence on European painting of the XVII Century and left traces even in the art of the great Dutchman, Rembrandt (the next room); the famous *Young Bacchus*, who in this canvas, from Olympian God became a young peasant; the *Sacrifice of Isaac*, an intensely dramatic scene captured in movement. Also represented in this room is Annibale Carracci, one of the masters of the Bolognese school, artist of *Venus with Satyr and Putti*, with the warm golden tones of obvious Venetian influence.

**Room 44.** *Rembrandt.* Of the great Dutch master's works there are shown the *Portrait of an Old Man*, a thoughful idealization of senility, and two self-portraits, one when young and one at a more mature age; the latter sad and resigned, very different from the other with its youthful impudent air. Along the walls a rich collection of Flemish and Dutch masters, specialists in Still Lifes, landscapes, lively *glimpses of life*, in precious ebony frames, which aim at recreating an old-fashioned small picture gallery. The *View with Copper Mine* by Civetta is celebrated; as is the limpid view of the *Groote Markt* of Harlem by Gerrit Berckheyde; Rachel Ruysch and Jan van Huysum are present with two extremely realistic *Still Lifes.*

**Room 45.** *Dedicated to the XVIII Century.* This room presents a panorama of the painting of this century, from the Venetians to the French, and to the Spanish Goya. By the great decorator Giovan Battista

Fig. 65 - Guardi: View fo Venice
Fig. 66 - Caravaggio: Medusa
Fig. 67 - Caravaggio: Young Baccus

**Fig. 68 - Rembrandt: Portrait of an Old Man**

Tiepolo, the beautiful ceiling represents *The Erection of a Statue to an Emperor,* of great scenographic effect; Guardi and Canaletto, the major Venetian landscape artists are present along with Longhi, painter of the delightful genre pictures. Outstanding pictures in the French section include *The Girl with the Shuttlecock* and *The Boy with Cards* by Chardin and the *Portrait of Marie Adelaide of France in Turkish Dress* by Liotard, a work which already announces the nineteenth century realism. Francisco Goya is the artist of the large portrait of the *Countess of Chinchon* standing, where the realism is associated with the lightness of the garment without pity for the physiognomy.

*The Vasariano Corridor.* Built in 1565, in only five months, as a private passage joining Palazzo Vecchio to the Pitti Palace, this corridor is almost one kilometre long. It is only opened by appointment and for group visits: there are about seven hundred works shown and divided into various sections. In the first tract, up to the Ponte Vecchio, there are various works of the Italian school between the XVII and XVIII Century.

On the Ponte Vecchio and beyond, is the *Collection of Selfportraits* (the most important in the world) begun by Cardinal Leopoldo dei Medici, who is portrayed here in the statue by Foggini. Some hundreds of works from the XIV Century to the present day are shown; from the Giotto school to Chagall. In the tract which comes out into the Boboli Gardens, there follows the Iconographic Collection, an immensely rich series of portraits of historical personages.

## CHURCH OF ORSANMICHELE (fig. 69)

(On Via Calzaiuoli, near Signoria Square; map of monuments n.9)

It was the former oratory of San Michele in Orto. In 1290 Arnolfo di Cambio built the «Loggia del Grano» (Grain Market), destroyed by a fire (1304). The cube shaped church, typical example of Florentine Gothic, was built by Francesco Talenti and Neri di Fioravanti (1337-1404), who built the grain lodge in the upper floors, in case of famine or siege of the city, now a hall used for periodic expositions by the Superintendant of Arts. In 1387 Simone Talenti closed the arches on the ground floor of the church in order to make the famous niches containing the statues of the patron saints of the Florentine guilds.

**Fig. 69 - Church of Orsanmichele - Lower floors**

The main entrance is from Via dell'Arte della Lana, but one can enter from the small door facing Via Calzaiuoli, from where, beginning from left to right, we can admire: 1) Tabernacle of the Mercanti di Calimala (Guild of Foreign Wool Merchants) — *St. John the Baptist* by Ghiberti (1414-1416), with harmonious late-Gothic rhythm; 2) Tabernacle of the Tribunal of the Merchants, by Donatello and Michelozzo: famous bronze group of the *Incredulity of St. Thomas* by Andrea del Verrocchio (1464-1483); above, medallion by Luca della Robbia. 3) Tabernacle of the Judges and Notaries: *St. Luke,* by Giambologna (1601). North side, Via Orsanmichele, 1) Tabernacle of the Butchers: *St. Peter,* young work by Donatello (1408-1413). 2) Tabernacle of the Tanners Guild: *St. Philip,* by Nanni di Banco (1409-1411). 3) Tabernacle of the Carpenters and Masons: *Four crowned Saints* and relief representing architects and

Figs. 70-71 - Orcagna: Tabernacle, Death and Assumption of the Virgin

sculptors, work of Nanni di Banco (1408); above medallion by Luca della Robbia. 4) Tabernacle of the Armourers and Sword makers, statue in bronze of *St. George,* copy of the original in marble by Donatello, preserved in the National Museum. Observe on the base, *St. George who frees the Princess* by Donatello, highly pictorial bas-relief. On the right, *Palace of the Arte della Lana* (Guild of the Wool Workers), restored in 1905 for the Dante Society, and joined to the upper floors of the church by means of the corridor. This tower house was the seat of the powerful Wool Guild, that employed about 30,000 workers and had 200 shops. The tabernacle on the corner with the *Incoronation of the Virgin,* XIV cent. work by Jacopo del Casentino, was transferred here in 1895, following the demolition of the old center. Following on the west side, facing Via Arte della Lana: 1) Tabernacle of the Moneychangers: *St. Matthew,* bronze by Ghiberti (1420). Over the main door of the church, sculpture by Nicolò Lamberti. 2) Tabernacle of the Wool Workers: *St. Stephen,* bronze by Ghiberti (1426). 3) Tabernacle of the Blacksmiths: *St. Eligius,* by Nanni di Banco (1415); on the base an episode in the life of the Saint is represented.

South side facing Via de' Lamberti: 1) Tabernacle of the Linen Workers: *St. Mark,* powerful work of Donatello (1408-1413). 2) Tabernacle of the Furriers; statue of *St. James,* perhaps work of Nicolò di

83

**Figs. 72-73 - Daddi: Madonna - Sangallo: St. Ann, Madonna and Child**

Pietro Lamberti, in the bas-relief, *Beheading of the Saint,* attributed to Ciuffagni. 3) Tabernacle of the Doctors and Apothecaries, by Simone Talenti; *Madonna of the Roses* perhaps by Simone Ferrucci. 4) Tabernacle of the Silk-workers and Goldsmiths: *St. John the Evangelist,* bronze by Baccio da Montelupo (1515). Above, in the *Medallion,* putto and crest of this guild, by Andrea della Robbia, beloved nephew and faithful pupil of Luca, father of Giovanni.

**Interior of the Church** (fig. 70), rectangular shaped, conserved in its original structure, illuminated by XV cent. stained glass windows. Solid pilasters, with frescoed heads, support the harmonious vaults and separate the aisles. In the right aisle is the famous *Tabernacle* by Andrea di Cione called Orcagna (1349-59). This admirable Gothic work terminates on high with the little cupola with the relief of the Saviour. The altar, with small twisted columns is adorned with panels on the bottom, and enriched with polychrome mosaic scenes from the *life of the Virgin.* On the back of the altar is a large scene of the *Death and Ascension of the Virgin* (fig. 71) by Orcagna, of obvious Sienese inspiration. The small spiraled columns and the *Angels carrying candelabras* of the parapet are by Pietro del Migliore (1366). The altar-piece with the famous *Madonna and Child* (fig. 72) is by Bernardo Daddi (1366).

**Fig. 74 - Piazza del Duomo with the Baptistry, Giotto's Bell-Tower, the Cathedral (St. Mary of the Flower). In the background the Dome designed by Brunelleschi.**

On the altar, to the left, *St. Ann with the Virgin and Child* (fig. 73), marble group by Francesco da Sangallo (1526).
Going out on to Via Calzaiuoli, on the opposite side of the street is the

CHURCH OF S. CARLO DEI LOMBARDI, attributed to Neri di Fioravante and Benci di Cione.

Inside, on the high altar is a *Deposition* by Nicolò di Pietro Gerini (end of XIV cent.). Continuing on the left of Via Calzaiuoli (widened in 1842) we reach the nearby Piazza del Duomo where, on the corner, is the beautiful LOGGIA DEL BIGALLO, jewel of Florentine architecture, attributed to Arnoldi (1352). The wrought-iron gate is by the Sienese Petrucci (1358). Inside the Loggia is a tabernacle with the *Madonna, Child and Angels* by Noferi (1515). In the lunette (on the Baptistry side) *Madonna and Child* by Alberto Arnoldi (1361).

### PIAZZA DUOMO (Cathedral Square)

In this square, also incorporating S. Giovanni Square, which is the ideal religious center of the city, are located the Baptistry, the Cathedral and the beautiful Bell Tower (fig. 75). We point out that, for the civic numeration, the side of the Baptistry and the Archiepiscopal Palace is S. Giovanni Square, while the side of the Cathedral, Bell Tower and Misericordia is Piazza Duomo.

### THE BAPTISTRY

Dedicated to St. John the Baptist, patron of the city. This splendid Romanesque building of the XI cent. that Dante called "the beautiful St. John", covered with white and green marble, is enriched by three magnificent bronze doors. The usual entrance is on South side. In order to follow the stylistic evolution of the sculpture of the three doors, we suggest they be visited in the order shown ahead.

**Interior.** Octagonal, harmonious and solemn, faced, as on the esterior, with green and white marble (fig. 75). The cupola is enriched with *mosaics* that are also used in the vault of the apse, added in the XIII cent. Solid and old columns, some of porphyry, support the trabeated architecture. Above is the gallery with exquisite mullioned windows that, with the lantern, illuminate the interior. In the cupola let us admire the famous mosaics, begun by Jacopo Francescano (1225) and continued by Venetian and Florentine artists, among whom is believed to be the young Cimabue who, beginning with the cartoons for these mosaics, laid the basis of Florentine painting.

Particularly interesting is the large and majestic figure of the *Saviour in the Final Judgement.* Represented in the other areas are *celestial Hierarchies;* episodes of the Bible among which are the *Creation of Adam and Eve, Stories of Joseph* and of *St. John the Baptist,* patron saint of Florence.

The large baptismal font that was in the center and where Dante was baptized, was dismantled in 1577. The fragments are conserved in the Museo del Duomo. Now baptism is performed at the small font against the wall, of the Pisan school (1371), surmounted by the *Baptism of Christ* by Allori (1590). Observe the area of the floor inlayed with motives of the Zodiac and oriental designs. On the opposite wall: *Tomb of the Antipope John XXIII* (Baldassare Cossa) deposed by the Council of Costance which recognized the sovereignty of Pope Martin V, who subsequently named him Cardinal of Florence, where he died in 1419. Cosimo the Elder, his great patron, commissioned Donatello to do this masterpiece which he executed with the help of other artists, among whom was Michelozzo, author of the exquisite figures of *Faith, Hope* and *Charity* in the lower niches.

To the left, monumental tablet to Bishop Ranieri (XII cent.). The altar of the tribune was reconstructed in the XII cent. The *angel candelabra is by Agostino di Jacopo (1320). At the back of the apse, Statue of the Baptist* by Piamontini (1688).

Fig. 75 - Baptistry - Interior
Fig. 76 - South Door - Andrea Pisano: Hope
Fig. 76 bis - North Door - Lorenzo Ghiberti: Annunciation

**Fig. 77 - Lorenzo Ghiberti: Second door of the Baptistry called "Gates of Paradise". Gilded bronze panel showing episodes from the Old Testament.**

**South Door.** By Andrea Pisano (da Pontedera) (1330-1336) who executed them following suggestions (it is believed) of Giotto, his teacher. The door has 20 panels with *Scenes from the Life of St. John the Baptist* and the *Cardinal and Theological Virtues.* They have symmetry and gothic rhythm as can be seen in the plastic and harmonious scenes of *Herod's Banquet* and the *Deposition of the Baptist in the Tomb* which, together with the panel representing *Hope* (fig. 76), announce the style of the first doors of Ghiberti, on the opposite side. The frames of the portal were later enriched with *leaves* and *graceful Angel's heads* by Vittorio Ghiberti, son and pupil of Lorenzo (1452-1462). Above the architrave,

1) Creation of Adam and Eve, Original Sin, Expulsion of Adam and Eve from the Garden of Eden; 2) Stories of Noah; 3) Stories of Jacob and Esau; 4)Moses receives the tablets of the law on Mt. Sinai; 5) Battle against the Philistines, David defeats Goliath; 6) Cain and Abel working the fields, Slaying of Abel; 7) The Apparition of the Angels to Abraham, Sacrifice of Isaac; 8) Joseph is sold to the Merchants, the gold cup is discovered in Benjamin's sack, Joseph makes himself known to his brothers; 9) The people of Israel cross the Jordan, the Battle of Jerico; 10) Solomon receives the Queen of Sheba at the Temple.

the *Beheading of St. John the Baptist* is by Vincenzo Danti (1572). Continuing to the left of the Baptistry, observe at the end of the Square, the Archiepiscopal Palace, built by Dosio (1572), rebuilt in 1895 to enlarge the square. From this side we can see the apse of the Baptistry, added in the XII cent. Farther ahead in the square, the *Column of St. Zenobius*, erected to commemorate the miracle of the Saint that, according to tradition, made a dead tree burst into flower when his remains passed by as they were being transferred from S. Lorenzo to the Duomo on January 23, 429.

**North Door** of the Baptistry. By Lorenzo Ghiberti (winner of the celebrated contest of 1402 in which great artists such as Jacopo della Quercia and Brunelleschi partecipated). Ghiberti, with the help of numerous collaborators, among whom Paolo Uccello and Donatello, began this first door in 1403, finishing them in 1424. The twenty upper panels narrate *Stories of the New Testament* while the lower eight represent *Evangelists and Doctors of the Church.* The most recent anti-traditional critics find in this door (ignored by many), more personal characteristics than in the second door, where the artist introduces the bas-relief inspired by Donatello. Here the scenes of rhythmic Gothic modulation, are rendered with more profound poetry as shown in the panels of the *Temptation and the Annunciation* (fig. 76 bis). Observe, in the frame work and the bands around the panels, the graceful heads of youths and adults. In the middle band on the left, the fifth head down from the top, with the turban, is a self portrait of Ghiberti. On the architrave, the bronze group of *John the Baptist preaching to a Pharisee and a Levite,* work of Gian Francesco Rustici (1506-1511), who shows the influence of Leonardo.

**Second Door.** Opposite the Cathedral, the second door called "Gate of Paradise" (fig. 77), was also done by Ghiberti (1425-1452) who completed it after 27 years of work, with the help of his son Vittorio, Bernardo Cennini, Michelozzo and other artists, including Benozzo Gozzoli. It is the door that Michelangelo judged worthy to be the Gate of Paradise. After the last war it was cleaned and brought back to its original gilded aspect.

In the panels of this famous work we can admire ample compositions rich with figures, architecture and landscape, done in bold, medium and bas-reliefs, typical of the great Renaissance era. The subjects of the ten panels, suggested by the humanist Leonardo Bruni, and taken from the *Old Testament* represent, beginning with the top left panel and reading from left to right:

1) Creation of Adam and Eve, Original Sin, Expulsion of Adam and Eve from the Garden of Eden; 2) Cain and Abel working the fields, Slaying of Abel; 3) Stories of Noah, rendered with richness of detail; 4) The Apparition of the Angels to Abraham, Sacrifice of Isaac; 5) Stories of Jacob and Esau particularly interesting for its architectural, plastic and Renaissance value; 6) Joseph is sold to the Merchants, the gold cup is discovered in Benjamin's sack, Joseph makes himself known to his brothers; 7) Moses receives the tablets of the Law on Mt. Sinai; 8) The people of Israel cross the Jordan, the Battle of Jericho; 9) Battle against the Philistines, David defeats Goliath; 10) Solomon receives the Queen of Sheba at the Temple.

In the framework of the door are graceful figures of Sibyls alternated with small heads portraying Florentine figures of the era. In the central vertical band, in the lower half, the small bald head is the selfportrait of a mature Ghiberti. On the architrave, the *Baptism of Christ* is by Andrea Sansovino 1502; the *Angel* is by Spinazzi (XVII cent.). At the sides of door are two old porphyre columns, donated to the Florentines by the Pisans (1117) for having faithfully defended their city while Pisa was at war in the Balearic Isles.

# THE CATHEDRAL - SANTA MARIA DEL FIORE
(Saint Mary of the Flower)

Arnolfo di Cambio began the construction (1296) to replace the old church of St. Reparata. After Arnolfo's death (1302), the work was continued by Giotto who died in 1337. Later (1357) Francesco Talenti and Giovanni di Lapo Ghini continued its construction, enlarging the original plan. In 1412 the name Santa Reparata was changed to S. Maria del Fiore (St. Mary of the Flower), alluding to the Florentine fleur-de-lys. In 1436 when Brunelleschi completed the cupola, the Church was consecrated by Pope Eugenius IV.

**Façade** by Emilio de Fabris (1881-88) is a cold XIX cent. imitation of Florentine Gothic, inspired by the decoration of sides of the Cathedral. The bronze doors with *Stories of the Virgin* are, by Passaglia (1897-1903) that on the left and the one in the center; and by Cassioli (1899), the door on the right.

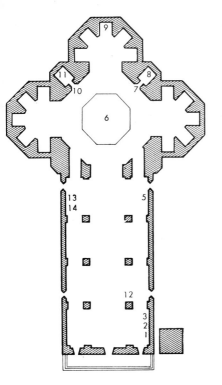

### PLAN OF THE CATHEDRAL
### (St. Mary of the Flower)

1. Bust of Brunelleschi
2. Statue of Isaiah, by Nanni di Banco (1408)
3. Bust of Giotto
4. Holy water basin (1380). The Angel and the basin are copies of the original in the Duomo Museum
5. Bust of Marsilio Ficino
6. Choir
7. Terracotta by Luca Della Robbia
8. Old Sacristy
9. Reliquary of St. Zenobius (Lorenzo Ghiberti)
10. Bronze door and terracotta by Luca Della Robbia
11. New Sacristy
12. Entrance to the excavations of St. Reparata
13. Entrance to the dome
14. Domenico Michelino: Dante shedding light on Florence with his Divine Comedy (fig. 80)

**Fig. 78 - The Cathedral: Interior**

**Interior** (fig. 78). The church is in the form of a Latin cross and has nave and two aisles (length 153 meters, width 38 meters, width of the transept 90 meters). It is the third longest church in the world after St. Peter's in Rome and St. Paul's in London. The first impression of nude simplicity devoid of any decoration, gives way to admiration for the controlled and measured proportions, which differ from other nordic cathedrals. The vertical surge of the vaults is broken by the gallery that runs above the arches continuing under the cupola and along the transept. The space in the arms of the transept is enriched by lateral domed chapels.

The very ample and architecturally well defined space, is sustained by simple and solid pilasters, typical example of Italianized Gothic. The light penetrates from the large rose window of the central nave and through the tall slim windows of the aisles.

Limiting ourselves to the most important works, we point out, on the internal façade: Stained glass window, following a design by Ghiberti. Around the clock are heads of Prophets by Paolo Uccello. In the right aisle, *bust of Brunelleschi,* work of Buggiano his student and heir. *Wooden tabernacle with Statue of a Prophet* by Nanni di Banco (1408). *Bust of Giotto,* by Benedetto da Maiano. Recently, remains of the pre-existent church of Santa Reparata were brought to light. The walls,

Fig. 79 - Michelangelo: Pietà - At present in the Museum of the Cathedral Institution

some frescoes, pieces of a wall decoration in brick and little columns, monumental slabs of the early XIV cent. and the Tomb of Filippo Brunelleschi were found. Farther ahead in the right aisle, in the niche near the side door is the *Bust of the Philosopher Marsilio Ficino* (d. 1499) by Andrea Ferrucci. The *octagonal marble Choir,* with bas-relief of *Apostles* and *Prophets* is a masterpiece by Bandinelli and helpers (1555). The *Wooden Crucifix* above is by Benedetto da Maiano. On the solid wings of the transept with its massive pillars, Brunelleschi's cupola rises elegantly and majestically (height 114 meters), inspiring that of Rome and of St. Paul's in London. The ingenious artists, after studying the monuments of ancient Rome, including the Pantheon, realized this splendid cupola with a new spirit, conserving however the Gothic idea that Arnolfo certainly had in mind when he projected the XIII century construction.

With machines of his own invention, Brunelleschi hauled the material to the top and built the octagonal cupola; two vaults separated by an airspace (as shown in the diagram-design A) that, solidly sustained by the play of weight and counter-weight, rises ever higher "between the sky and the earth". The decoration of the interior was supposed to be mosaic but was unfortunately altered by Vasari and Zuccari who frescoed the pompous and manneristic *Final Judgement* (1572-79). The magnificent *stained glass windows* around the base of the dome were made from cartoons by Donatello, Paolo Uccello, Ghiberti and Andrea del Castagno. In the niches of the wings around the choir are figures of *Apostles* by XV cent. sculptors; among the most notable, *St. James* by Jacopo Sansovino. On the right of the choir is the *door to the old Sacristy.* In the lunette, the *Ascension* in glazed terracotta, by Luca della Robbia (c. 1450).

At the back of the apse (n. 9 on the plan), under the altar (often covered), is the famous bronze reliquary by Ghiberti (1442), with the *Miracle of St. Zenobius who Resuscitates a Child in the Presence of its Mother and Onlookers.* Above the altar, a mediocre *Last Supper* by Balducci (XVI cent.). Returning towards the transept one can admire the architectural complex of the church. On the right, the bronze door of the new Sacristy, by Luca Della Robbia, with pamels representing: the *Madonna and Child with Evangelists and Doctors of the Church.* Observe the self-portrait of the artist in the small bald head below. The splendid *Resurrection* in the lunette, of glazed terracotta, is also a masterpiece by Luca della Robbia.

**Interior of the Sacristy.** Contains cabinets with inlay decoration enriched with festoons, due in great part to the da Maiano brothers. There are two marble lavaboes by Buggiano (1440): the delicate *angel's head* on the right one is attributed to Mino da Fiesole. Lorenzo the Magnifi-

Fig. 80 - Domenico Michelino: Dante presenting the "Divine Comedy", indicating the door to the Inferno

Fig. 80 bis - View of the excavations of St. Reparata. The crypt contains different rests of the primitive palaeochristian church and the graves of the cathedral's architects.

cent found shelter in this Sacristy while his brother Giuliano fell under the assassin's knife, in the Pazzi Conspiracy (Easter 1478).

On the floor in the center of the transept, observe the *Gnomon* represented by the metal disc that was placed here in 1450 by Toscanelli for the purpose of controlling the center of gravity of the cupola on the day of the summer solstice. Continuing along the right aisle, before the side door, is a small door at the entrance to the Cupola. For aesthetic reasons it is not permitted to install an elevator for a comfortable ascent to the cupola but, to those that are able, we do suggest climbing the interesting spiral stair-case to admire, from above, the beautiful geometric polychromed marble floor of the church, by Baccio d'Agnolo (1526), the ingenious internal construction of the cupola, and the vast panorama of the city and its surrounding hills. Continuing our walk in the church, on the wall, *Dante shedding light on Florence with his Divine Comedy,* a painting by Domenico Michelino (fig. 80), pupil of Fra' Angelico (plate XL). Farther ahead are two admirable *equestrian portraits* of the Florentine Republic's most faithful generals; *John Hawkwood,* by Paolo Uccello (1436) who inspired Andrea del Castagno (1456), painter of the other General, *Nicolò da Tolentino.* The two frescoes at

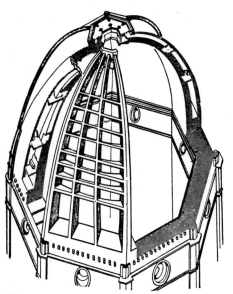

Brunelleschi, friend of the astronomer Toscanelli, after his profound mathematical studies and attentive observations of ancient buildings, especially the Pantheon in Rome, built the first cupola without use of the customary scaffolding. As shown in the sketch, his creation is a double dome, the outer one having enormous ribs. Below, big robust pilasters around the tribune prepare the remarkable thrust of the cupola, that rises elegantly and majestically on high.

one time were on the internal façade, but then were restored, transferred on to canvas, and displayed here in the better light.

In the last bay is a *bust* of Arnolfo di Cambio (1843); in the wooden tabernacle, statue of a prophet and a portrait of the humanist Poggio Bracciolini (school of Donatello). Finally, *a bust of Emilio de Fabris,* the architect of the façade, by Consani (1887)..

Among the events that took place in this Cathedral we remember: the Council of Florence, that reconciled the Greek and Latin churches under the patronage of Cosimo the Elder (1429). During the Lenten season of 1497, Savonarola gave his memorable sermons, which influenced the course of Florentine history and the artists of the time.

# GIOTTO'S BELL-TOWER

Giotto's Campanile was erected on line with the façade of the Cathedral and enriched with white, pink and green marble. It is 84,75 meters in height and has a staircase with 416 steps. It is a splendid example of Florentine Gothic architecture, on a square base with solid side pillars. It was begun by Giotto in 1334, who completed the first zone. After his death (1337) it was continued by his pupil Andrea Pisano who worked on the two upper stories with the beautiful mullioned windows. In 1348 he was succeeded by Talenti who finished it in 1359. There is still discussion about Giotto's original project terminating with cusps that Talenti changed by ending with a panoramic terrace that has an open-work parapet and a jutting cornice resting on corbelling and trilobated arches. In order to have a better look at the bell-tower we suggest you stand at a distance from where you can see the highest window, placed in the arch of the cusp, that harmonizes with the small door on the bottom. The statues of Saints and Prophets, including Donatello's *Abacus,* that were once in the niches, are now conserved in the Cathedral Museum, together with the panels of the base representing *Scenes from Genesis* and the *Activities* of *Man,* by Andrea Pisano following designs by Giotto, which have been substituted with plaster models.

To the right of the Bell-tower across the street:

# SEAT AND ORATORY OF THE MISERICORDIA

Among the oldest congregations in Italy, this was founded by a simple porter for the purpose of transporting the sick to hospitals. The "brothers", who belong to all circles, take turns, without compensation, in offering, this service and other works of charity.

**Exterior of the Cathedral.** Moving along on this side of the street, we can better admire the "beautiful" Bell-tower and the majestic architectural complex of the cathedral, enlarged in the course of the centuries, as shown by the splendid mullioned windows of which the smaller and lower ones on the left obviously belong to the original plan. Among the most beautiful **portals** on this side, we point out the one on the right near the cupola called of the "Canonici", by Lorenzo di Giovanni d'Ambrogio and Piero di Giovanni Tedesco. In the lunette the *Madonna and Child* is by Lorenzo di Giovanni d'Ambrogio who, with Nicolò Lamberti, also sculpted the two *Angels*. We suggest you proceed towards Via del Proconsolo and Via dell'Oriuolo, in order better to admire the Bell-tower, the solid base of the Cupola, and the gallery that runs along only one section of it, by Baccio d'Agnolo, left incomplete because it was criticized by Michelangelo, who defined it a "cricket cage". On the corner of Via Oriuolo is the beautiful *Strozzi of Mantova Palace* (XVI cent.) with its rusticated stone, beautiful windows and splendid portals.

Continuing around the square we see the entrance to the Cathedral Museum that we describe below. Also observe the portals of the "workshops" that numbered many in this square. Among these is that of Donatello indicated by the modern bust in the niche. After Via dei Servi, observe, on the side of the Cathedral, the famous door called of the "mandorla" (almond) because of the shape of the niche containing the beautiful sculpture of the *"Assumption"*, by Nanni di Banco. The small figures of *Prophets* on the long pilasters are believed to be by the young Donatello. The mosaic representing the "Annunciation" is by Domenico Ghirlandaio with the help of his brother David. Retracing our steps to n. 9 Piazza Duomo, we arrive at the entrance to the

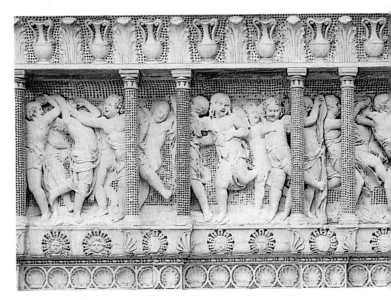

**Fig. 81 - Museum of the Opera del Duomo - Donatello: Choir - loft (detail)**

**Fig. 82 - Museum of the Opera del Duomo - Donatello: Habakkuk**

**Fig. 83 - The Magdalen (detail)**

## MUSEO DELL'OPERA DEL DUOMO (Cathedral Museum)
(Saint Mary of the Flower)

In the niche above the entrance is a *bust of Cosimo I,* work of Bandini (1572). Access to the Museum is through the atrium. Opposite the entrance, in the small corridor, one find fragments of sculptures, and some panels of the old baptismal font where Dante was baptised, and which at one time was in the Baptistery.

In the large rectangular room are works by Arnolfo di Cambio (d.1302), architect and sculptor, including, on the left, the statue of *Pope Boniface VIII* with his arm raised in blessing, and on the opposite wall, statues that were on the old façade of the Cathedral. Against the right wall, among other statues is Donatello's *St. John the Evangelist,* that is supposed to have inspired Michelangelo with his Moses. On the wall, observe the design for the old façade of the Cathedral, dismantled in the XVI cent.

From the left hand side of the statue of Boniface VIII one passes to three small rooms dedicated to the funeral mask of Brunelleschi and the models of the Dome; various ancient machines used in the work on the Cathedral are also found here. The room with the ancient façade opens into that dedicated to models of the Cathedral façades over the centuries, with precious missals and a large lectern, and from here to the small chapel containing rare reliquaries and holy vestments. A short staircase leads to the landing with the famous *Pietà* by Michelangelo (1550, Fig. 79) which was intended to be placed on his tomb. This is an unfinished work of intense dramatic feeling. Joseph of Arimathea, supporting Christ, is believed to be a selfportrait of Michelangelo. Perhaps because he was not satisfied with it, the artist broke up the group which was put together again by his pupil Calcagni, who finished the figure of the Magdalen. Go from here up to the:

**Figs. 84-85 - Museum of the Opera del Duomo - Luca della Robbia: Choir - loft (detail)**

**First Floor**, dedicated to the famous choir lofts by Luca della Robbia (1428-31) and Donatello (1433-39) (fig. 81). On the left, above, is the plaster reconstruction of Luca's cantoria with *figures of children singing psalm 31 of David.* Below are the dismantled original panels (figs.84-85). On the right wall is *Donatello's choir loft* with dancing putti, rendered impetuous and spontaneous, in their natural and naïve mannerisms. Below, also by Donatello, the impressive penitent *Magdalen* in polychrome wood (1460), of a crude realism. It has been restored after the damage suffered during the floods in 1966 when it was exhibited in the Baptistery. On the walls are *Florentine tapestries* with Stories of *St. John the Baptist,* from cartoons by Alessandro Allori (XVI cent.). Among the statues originally in the niches of the Bell-tower notice, against the end wall, the famous Abakuk (fig. 82) by Donatello. On the right we enter the room with the famous silver altar, once in the Baptistry, a masterpiece by XV cent. Florentine artists. In the center of the altar are *episodes of the life of the Baptist* by Cennini and the figure of *St. John* by Michelozzo. On the left side the *Birth of St. John* by Antonio Pollaiuolo and the *Visitation* by Bernardo Cennini. On the right side, *Herod's Banquet* by Antonio Salvi and *Beheading of the Saint* by Verrocchio. In this room also are precious embroideries with 27 little scenes of the *Life of Christ* and, in the showcase against the entrance wall is a rare Byzantine mosaic with scenes of *Christ's Life* (XIII cent.).

In the centre of the room, one can admire two panels of the Door of Paradise, which were placed here after the careful restoration which brought to light the original gilding. They represent: The *Battle against the Philistines* and *David killing Goliath* (bottom left hand side of the door); *Joseph sold to the Merchants*; the Gold Goblet rediscovered in Benjamin's bag, and Joseph recognised by his brothers (in the centre on the right of the door).

Returning to the room with the Choir-lofts, we pass into the small room dedicated to the famous panels, originally on the Bell-tower, by Andrea Pisano. It is believed that some of the preparatori designs for these panels were furnished by Giotto. Notice the ones of *"Agriculture"* and *"Drunkenness of Noah"* that reveal the superior personality of Giotto as a sculptor.

# SECOND ITINERARY

*Church of San Lorenzo, Laurentian Library, Medici Chapels - Medici - Riccardi Palace - Church of St. Mark, Museum of St. Mark, of Angelico - Academy Gallery, Tribune of David - Conservatory of Music «Cherubini» - Museo delle Pietre Dure (Museum and work shop of semi-precious stones).*

(This itinerary is indicated on the monumental map by the numbers 4, 5, 7, and 8).

## CHURCH OF SAN LORENZO

In the square (fig. 86, city plan 4), on a beautiful base, is the *monument* to Giovanni father of Cosimo I, by Bandinelli (1540), with the unusual figure of a seated general. This monument touched the wittiness of the Florentines, who coined the famous epigram: Messer Giovanni delle Bande Nere, "annoyed, and tired from his long journey, dismounted from his horse and took a seat". Notice the base, more interesting than the statue, adorned with Medicean heraldic motives. The Church was commissioned by Cosimo the Elder (in the place of a preexisting church believed to have been founded by St. Ambrose) near his Palace, as a parish church and Medicean cemetery. It is the first Renaissance

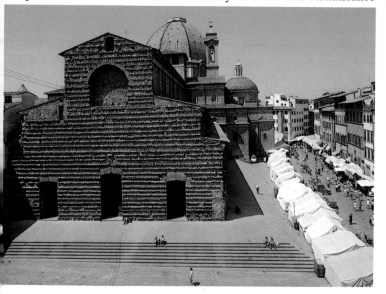

**Fig. 86 - Church of San Lorenzo and the Medici Chapels**

church, begun by Brunelleschi in 1419 (upon return from his studies of Roman basilicas) and finished by his pupil Manetti. Later Michelangelo made a project for the façade but it was never carried out.

By Michelangelo is the internal façade of the church and the famous Laurentian Library in the cloister. The bell-tower is by Ruggeri (1746).

**Interior.** In the form of a Latin cross with a nave and two aisles and a wide transept with chapels along the walls. The wide central nave with the panelled ceiling and the geometrically patterned floor, is illuminated by large rectangular windows. In the aisles with the cross-vaulted ceiling, the light enters through small round windows.

This harmonious basilica is a triumph of Brunelleschi's perpective vision. The grey stone ribs and columns, with their capitals topped by elegant abacuses that support the round arches, perfectly harmonize with the white plaster walls. At the end of the central nave, as seen on the plan marked nos. 2-3, are the famous *pulpits* by Donatello, made in collaboration with his helpers Bertoldo and Bellano, with panels representing the Passion of Christ. Particularly interesting is the *Deposition* in the left pulpit, the last work of the artist, rendered with profound humanity. At the head of the right transept (behind the pulpit, no.4 on the plan), is an exquisite *tabernacle* with graceful "putti" by Desiderio da Settignano, which was the inspiration for many other famous Florentine tabernacles.

In the chapel of the right transept is the tomb of the Naturalist Stenson. (We point out that the Main Chapel was shortened when the Chapel of the Princes was built, attaching it to the church, as described below (see plan).

**Main Altar**, enclosed by a balustrade. The altar is decorated with semiprecious stones. The marble *Crucifix* is by Baccio da Montelupo, pupil of Michelangelo. In front of the balustrade observe the metal gratings marking the place under which Cosimo the Elder (d. 1464) is buried. Next to him is buried Donatello, of whom Cosimo was a great patron and admirer.

At the head of the left transept a large but overpowering fresco of the Martyrdom of St. Lawrence by Bronzino, who, having returned from Rome, wanted to emulate Michelangelo's art in the Vatican. The beautiful *Choir-loft* inlaid with quartz and polychrome marble is attributed to Donatello. In the chapel to the left, *St. Joseph in his workshop with the Child Jesus,* work of intense humanity by Annigoni, the famous portrait painter of Popes and Sovereigns. In the last chapel of this left transept is the *Monument to the Countess Moltk Ferrari Corbelli* by Duprè (1864). On the left we enter the

**Old Sacristy,** by Brunelleschi (1420-29) is square in shape and the light penetrates from the lantern of the little cupola and from the large lateral lunettes. The apse, with its fine marble balustrade, has an altar made by Donatello's pupils, following the master's design.

The cupola is enriched, high up frescoed ed *Signs of the Zodiac.*

On two sides of the apse are: two *Doors* with small ionic columns and a triangular tympanum by Donatello into which the artist inserted his valuable bronze doors with panels representing *the Apostles and Doctors of the Church* rendered intensely dramatic. By this great sculptor, who was also a friend and collaborator of Brunelleschi, we can admire: the *Stories of St. John the Evangelist,* in the pendentives; *the Four Evangelists,* in terracotta in the lunettes; and the lively *Cherubs* around the trabeation.

Donatello also modelled the famous and realistic *Bust of St. Lawrence* in terracotta (on the right cabinet), which was probably the portrait of a young Florentine boy. In the little room on the left of the apse is a magnificent *lavabo* with an *eagle* with spread wings. In the center of the Sacristy, a large marble table which covers the *sarcophagus of Giovanni dei Medici and his wife Piccarda,* parents of Cosimo the Elder, by Andrea Cavalcanti (1434). Near the exit is a splendid porphyry *Sarcophagus* with bronze decorations and an esquisite marble cornice, surmounted by ample bronze tracery that divides the wall and enriches the *Tomb of*

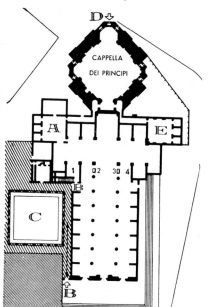

**PLAN OF THE CHURCH OF S. LAURENCE AND OF THE MEDICEAN CHAPELS**

A. Old Sacresty (Brunelleschi)

B. Entry to the Cloister

C. Cloister of Brunelleschi where, at the bottom, on the right, there is the staircase leading to the famous Laurenziana Library of Michelangelo.

D. Madonna Square from where, on the left, one enters the Medicean Chapels.

E. New Sacristy (Michelangelo)

1. Martelli Chapel

2-3. Pulpits by Donatello

4. Tabernacle of Desiderio da Settignano

Fig. 87 - Laurentian Library - Michelangelo: Triple Staircase of the Vestibule

Fig. 88 - Brunelleschi: Cloister of the Church of San Lorenzo

*Giovanni and Piero dei Medici* (sons of Cosimo the Elder), by Verrocchio (1472).

Returning to the church, on the right (no. 1 in the plan), is the

**Martelli Chapel**: on the altar is an *Annunciation* by Fra Filippo Lippi. Against the right wall, monument to Donatello by Romanelli (1896). On the left wall, *Sarcophagus of the Martelli Family.* Opening the door on the façade, we enter the beautiful *Cloister* in the style of Brunelleschi (fig. 88). In the corner is the statue of *Paolo Stovio* by Francesco da Sangallo. The brief staircase leads to the first floor with its splendid portico and Florentine roof. By walking around the entire portico we can better admire the vast architectural complex of San Lorenzo. To the right of the square is the entrance to the famous

**Laurentian Library**, open (save changes) weekdays from 9 to 17 h. Free entrance. It is closed on holidays. When the church is closed one can enter the Library from the door on the left side of the church. The library contains valuable works collected by Cosimo the Elder and Lorenzo the Magnificent, for which Pope Clement VII wanted to build a worthy seat thus commissioning Michelangelo (1524) to erect this famous Library.

**Vestibule.** One of this great artist's most original creations, in which the architectural planes are animated with dramatic dynamism, with double columns enclosing the limited walls, which in turn are deeply excavated by the wide windows. The TRIPLE STAIRCASE (fig. 87), designed by the Master, was finished by Vasari in 1558.

**Library** (fig. 87). Daring and austere in its extremely regular form: it is, in fact, a large rectangle. In the double rows of stalls are rare and notable *Latin and Greek* manuscripts of the VI to the XVI centuries. Among the most famous documents are the celebrated *Pandects* and the V cent. *Virgil.* The beautiful floor is by Tribolo, following Michelangelo's design. The beautiful two-colored windows are by Giovanni da Udine.

Returning to Piazza San Lorenzo, to the left of the Church, walking along the animated Via dell'Ariento with its numerous stalls, we can see ahead to the central Market, by Mengoni (1847).
As shown on the map, continuing on the left of the Canto dei Nelli, we reach Piazza Madonna where, on the left, is the entrance to the famous.


## MEDICI CHAPELS

From the entrance vestibule we immediately enter the vast *Medici Crypt.* The numerous inscriptions on the tombs indicate the burial places of the *Grand Dukes and members of the Medici family. Cosimo I his wife Eleonor of Toledo and their children* are buried in the first vault on the right. His father, *Giovanni dalle Bande Nere,* a great soldier, is buried near the center; the last Medici, Anna Maria Ludovica, who died in 1743, is buried near the last pilaster at the right hand end. (In the end vault, some members of the Lorraines, successors to the Medici, are buried). The staircase leads to the grand

**Chapel of the Princes** (fig. 89). It was begun by Nigetti (1604) on a design by Don Giovanni dei Medici, natural son of Cosimo I. This Chapel (left incomplete) was commissioned by the Grand Duke Ferdinand I Medici who wanted to glorify his House. It is a vast octagon with a cupola (height 52 meters), with the walls encrusted with rare marble and semi-precious stones. The *Cupola,* that originally was supposed to be made of lapislazuli, was later frescoed by Pietro Benvenuti (1829) with stories of the *Creation* and the *Final Judgement.* The six sarcophagi are dedicated to the Grand Dukes buried below in the crypt. Only two niches have colossal gilded bronze statues by Pietro Tacca (XVII cent.). The other niches remained incomplete. Around the walls, on the base, are represented the sixteen coats-of-arms of Florence and other Tuscan cities (figs. 90-91). The altar and floor are modern. Behind the altar are two small rooms with precious and rare reliquaries.

**Fig. 89 - Chapel of the Medici Princess (San Lorenzo)**
**Figs. 90-91 - Coats of arms of Florence and Pisa (mosaics)**

**Fig. 92 - Michelangelo: Night (Monument to Giuliano Medici)**

Returning to the entrance, the small corridor leads to the
**New Sacristy**, begun by Michelangelo in 1520. It was commissioned by
the Popes Leo X and Clement VII, to hold the remains of their fathers,
Lorenzo the Magnificent and Giuliano (assassinated in the Pazzi conspiracy), and other members of the Medici family. Michelangelo
worked on it in periods until 1537. With the fall of the Republic, Michelangelo went to Rome where he died in 1564. (His body was brought to
Florence and buried in St. Croce). The Chapel, continued by Vasari,
was left incomplete. The highly suggestive effect of the construction is
due to the cupola placed on a square base, that develops Brunelleschi's
themes, with its grey stone ribs against white walls, reinforced by marble
structures at the base. Entering, on the left: Tomb of Lorenzo, Duke of
Urbino (fig.94) (see geneaological tree), called the *Thinker*, because he
is represented in profound meditation. The statues on the sarcophagus
represent: *Dusk* and *Dawn*, who, in their unfinished state, are highly
plastic and dramatic and suggest profound lyricism. Also buried in this
tomb is his son Duke Alessandro, brother of Catherine dei Medici, last
of the branch of Cosimo the Elder, assassinated by his cousin Lorenzino (1537).
Against the right wall, *Tomb of Giuliano, Duke of Nemours* (1487-
1516), son of Lorenzo the Magnificent (fig. 95), idealized as a noble and
108

Fig. 93

strong general. The statues on the tomb: *Day* (incomplete) who is still wrapped in matter and fights to free himself (fig. 96). On the left is the famous *Night* (fig. 92), female figure, plastic and contracted in the immobility of the "after-life"; at the end of human existence, restless and tormented as was the artists own life.

Against the entrance wall, incomplete *tomb* of Lorenzo the Magnificent and his brother Giuliano, buried below, as the inscription reads. By Michelangelo is the *Madonna and Child* (fig. 93), sculptural group with complex "contrapposto" movement. The two lateral statues of *SS.*

**Figs. 94-95 - Michelangelo: Monuments to Lorenzo and Giuliano Medici**

*Cosmos and Damian,* patron saints of the Medici, are by followers of Michelangelo, Angelo Montorsoli and Raffaello da Montelupo. From the door on the left side of the altar one can go down to the crypt, a small but extremely evocative ambient, covered with drawings by Michelangelo and pupils. Apply to the custodian.

Returning to San Lorenzo Square, farther ahead, the short Via dei Gori (on the side of the Medici Palace) leads to the small Square of St. Giovannino degli Scolopi.
On the right, observe the beautiful *Façade* of the church of the same name that Ammannati built with his own money. The artist is buried in the interior of the church, to the left of the entrance, as recorded by the inscription. This square marks the end of Via Martelli and the beginning of Via Cavour (at one time called Via Larga), where we admire the Medici-Riccardi Palace.

Fig. 96 - Michelangelo: Day (Monument to Giuliano Medici)

## MEDICI-RICCARDI PALACE

This splendid Renaissance palace (fig. 97) typical example of a wealthy person's home, was built by Michelozzo (1440-60) for Cosimo the Elder. The *façade*, elegant and majestic with its stories of decreasingly rusticated ashlar, is finished at the top with a splendid classical cornice. The beautiful mullioned windows became examples for "Renaissance" architecture. Among the people who lived here were Cosimo the Elder, Lorenzo the Magnificent and his successors, among whom was Catherine dei Medici, the future Queen of France. Among the foreign Sovereigns were: Charles VIII of France and Charles V of Spain. In 1655 the Medici moved their home to the Pitti Palace and sold this palace to the Riccardi family, who enlarged it by seven windows per story and included the entrance to the stables, on Via Larga (today Via Cavour). Similar additions were made on the side facing Via Ginori. Later the Palace passed into the hands of the State and became the seat of the Prefecture.

**Courtyard**, with an arcade, and the upper Loggia closed with windows. The beautiful *medallions* in the architrave are attributed to Bertoldo, pupil of Donatello, and the *graffiti* are by Maso di Bartolomeo (1452).

Fig. 97

While the *first floor* has elegant double arched windows, the *second floor* presents an elegant "ionic collonade". Unfortunately the courtyard is overpowered by the decorations added by the Riccardi family, which should be removed. The statue of Orpheus is by Bandinelli. On the left in the first four rooms where Lorenzo the Magnificent had his apartments, temporary exhibitions are set up periodically. Through the glass door on the right we climb to the

**Chapel of Benozzo Gozzoli**, a pupil of Fra Angelico (1459-60). A painter of a pleasant narrative vein, in these celebrated frescoes, he glorified the Medici, against a background of the outskirts of Florence and the green Tuscan countryside. Singe the Chapel has no windows, the artist had to overcome this difficulty with the aid of artificial light. Entering, on the right wall we admire, the *Procession of the Wise Kings* (fig. 98) against the background of the luminous, steep hill of Vincigliata, between Fiesole and Settignano. Under the Oriental features and clothes of the Kings and their following, we can recognize Greek and Florentine personalities of the XV cent., who participated in the famous parade that was held on the occasion of the Council of 1439. It is believed that the artist was also inspired by the tournament of 1459 for the visit of Pius II, which saw the Medici in all their pomp and splendor. The first young horseman is supposed to be Lorenzo the Magnificent, idealized, with his gracious sisters Bianca Maria and Nannina. Among the people in the following, we recognize Piero Medici, among the first in the upper group , and in the corner, a *self portrait* of the artist, with his name on his hat. On the next wall: *John VII Emperor of Byzantium.* Followed on the other wall by *Joseph, Patriarch of Costantinople,* riding the mule. The Patriarch died during the Council and was buried in St. Maria Novella. In the handsome young man riding a Leopardi it is believed that the artist idealized *Giuliano,* the brother of Lorenzo the Magnificent. The splendid *ceiling, the stalls and the polychrome marble floors* were executed following designs by Michelozzo. On the altar a *Madonna and Child,* copy by Neri Bicci from an original by Fra Filippo Lippi, at one time on display here, now at the Berlin Museum. On the small walls of the altar, we can admire Gozzoli's *musical Angels,* against the beautiful Tuscan countryside where the Medici had their villas. Returning to the courtyard, the staircase on the right leads to the FIRST FLOOR, in the splendid rooms of the Prefecture. On the left and then to the right, we enter the famous *Rooms of Luca Giordano* (1682-83) where the artist of the same name frescoed the vault with the *Apotheosis of Cosimo III* with perspective effects. The *Room,* enriched with gil-

**Fig. 98 - Medici - Riccardi Palace (Chapel) - Benozzo Gozzoli: Procession of the Wise Kings (detail)**

ded mirrors, benches and seats, is now reserved for the Provincial Council that holds its reunions here.

Returning to Via Cavour, farther ahead on the right, we arrive at San Marco Square.

## SAN MARCO SQUARE (see city plan n. 7)

In the center of the square (fig. 99) is a mediocre bronze monument of General Manfredo Fanti by Pio Fedi (1873).

## CHURCH OF SAN MARCO

The original XII century construction was modified by Michelozzo and Sinvani. The façade is Baroque and is by Giovacchino Pronti (1780).

**Interior** has a single nave. In the center of the great carved ceiling is a *Madonna in Glory* by Pucci (XVIII cent.). Above the entrance is a large *Crucifix* from the Giotto school. Among the other works we remember: on the second altar of the right wall, *Madonna and Saints* by Fra Bartolomeo (1509); on the third altar, *large mosaic* of the VIII cent. representing the *Virgin Praying* (originally in the Oratory of Pope John VII in Rome). The next altar was inserted in the arch by Giambologna (1580), over which there is a statue of St. Zenobius, by the same artist.

**Main Chapel** by Silvani with frescoes representing the *Glory of the Dominican Order,* by Gherardini (1717); the *Last Supper* is of the Florentine school of the XVIII cent.; on the walls, *the Wedding of Cana* and the *Epiphany* frescoed by the French artist Parrocel (1702); on the left of the Main Chapel is the *Serragli Chapel* or of the "Sacrament", decorated with late XVI cent. paintings. On the left is the *Altar of Saint Antonino,* where the embalmed body of the Saint is preserved. On the wall of the left aisle are the *tombstones* of Giovanni Pico della Mirandola (1463-94) and of the humanist poet Agnolo Poliziano. Leaving the church, on the left is the entrance to San Marco Museum.

## SAN MARCO MUSEUM

The restoration of this complex was made possible by Cosimo the Elder, a great banker and politician of vast foresight who greatly protected the monastic orders, aware of their influence on the people,

**Fig. 99 - Square, Church and Museum of St. Mark**

whom he in turn tried to propitiate by every means possible. On his order, Michelozzo (1437-52), his favorite artist, restored the bell-tower and brought the fallen monastery back to its old splendor, after having been left vacant by the suppressed Salvestrine friars. Beato Angelico (Guido Guidolino di Pietro), born in Vicchio di Mugello 1387, who, at the age of twenty, became a friar in the Convent of San Domenico, transferred here with his fellow priests. He acquired his art from Lorenzo Monaco and the miniaturists that flourished in Florence. Later he turned his attention to the pictorial vision of Masaccio, and combined the compactness of forms to his own delicate color. Having become famous for his frescoes in Orvieto and the Vatican, in 1449 he was named Prior of San Marco and in 1452 of San Domenico where, as a young man, with his brother Benedetto, manuscript writer, he had renounced the pleasures of the world. He died in Rome in 1455 and was buried in St. Maria della Minerva. For his personality and his mystical art he was given the name Beato Angelico. In this monastery also lived Friar Antonio Pierozzi (1389-1445), acclaimed Bishop of Florence, later sanctified. Cosimo the Elder, appreciated his discussions and often left the palace and retired here where he had his private cell. Savonarola was called from Ferrara by Lorenzo the Magnificent and became Prior, and Bartolomeo della Porta, Renaissance painter and fervent follower of Savonarola entered the Dominican order. The Convent passed to the State in 1860. After 1920, with material collected from other sources, the Museum was constituted and entirely dedicated to B. Angelico.

**First Cloister** (fig. 100). A splendid example of Renaissance monastic architecture, with flower-beds and shaded by the beautiful cedar of Lebanon. This first cloister is called "of St. Antonino" because of the XVI century frescoes, with episodes from the life on the Bishop-Saint. At the end of the portico, in front of the entrance, *St. Dominic at the Foot of the Crucifix* by Angelico.

To the right, in a lunette, *St. Antonino acclaimed Bishop enters the Cathedral,* seen with the original façade destroyed in 1588, frescoed by Poccetti. In the lunette at the end, *Cosimo the Elder orders Michelozzo and Helpers to rebuilt the Convent.* In the lunette on the right, *Jesus dressed as a Pilgrim received by two Dominicans,* by Angelico. On the right:

**Old Hospice of the Pilgrims.** A large rectangular room, where Angelico's works have been displayed. The splendid collection clearly shows the evolution of the artist, who goes from the light and abstract tones of Lorenzo Monaco, and arrives at the Renaissance vision *(Madonna of the Linaioli,* cited below), in which he achieves great ef-

**Fig. 100 - St. Mark's - First Cloister**

fects of devotion. Against the long right wall: table with *Madonna and Child with Saints,* scenes from the *lives of SS. Cosmos and Damian;* the one of the *Burial* shows St. Mark's Square with the old Convent. Against the long left wall we can admire the panels, which once formed the doors of a tabernacle containing silver in the Sacristy of SS. Annunziata, with *Episodes in the life of the Virgin and Christ,* divided into 35 small scenes painted by Angelico and helpers, among whom is Baldovinetti. Among the most interesting, observe the *Flight into Egypt.* Farther ahead, *Final Judgement* (restored), where, among the Elect, Angelico glorified the Dominican order (fig. 101), while, among the Damned (work of helpers), are represented unworthy monks and prelates. The large *Deposition* (c. 1440, restored). The famous, delicate *Madonna of the Star* (c. 1430); and the exquisite *Annunciation* with, below, *Adoration of the Magi* that reveals Angelico as a fine miniaturist. Among the episodes of the Virgin rendered with intense religiousness, are *Scenes of Zacharius writing the name of the infant John,* while in the background opens an admirable view of a Tuscan villa.

On the wall at the far end, a large *Deposition* (c. 1435), rendered with intense humanity and strong religious feeling. In the *Joseph of Arimathea, with the black cap, holding the body of Christ,* he portrayed Michelozzo, the architect of the convent. In the pinnacles: *Noli me tangere, Resurrection, the Marys at the Sepulchre* by Lorenzo Monaco, teacher of

**Fig. 101 - Fra' Angelico - Final Judgement (detail)**

Angelico. Returning to the entrance wall, we admire the famous and large *Madonna of the Flax Workers,* expressed by Angelico in full Renaissance form, inside the beautiful frame by Ghiberti. In the leaves, *St. John the Baptist* and *St.Mark the Apostle*; in the predella *the Preaching of St. Peter, Adoration of the Magi* and *the Martyrdom of St. Mark.* Returning to the cloiser, at the end on the right,

**Lavatory.** The lunette seen here with the fresco of "Saint Peter Martyr Calls for Silence" by Angelico, was at one time above the door to the Sacristy, and the relative designs. The next room is dedicated to Fra Bartolomeo, Renaissance painter active in this convent (1472-1517), by whom we may admire some minor works and the majestic, incomplete *Madonna and Child,* with Leonardo style shading.

On the right:

**Old Refectory of the Salvestrines.** On the right wall is a large fresco, deteriorated with time, by Fra Bartolomeo and Albertinelli, representing the *Final Judgement.* Ahead is a Baroque pulpit. On the end wall, fresco by Sogliani (XVI cent.) of the *Crucifix,* and below, *Episodes from the life of St. Dominic* who, left without provisions, prays with his friars and receives aid from the Angels; on the sides *St. Anthony and St. Catherine of Siena.* Coming back to the cloister, ahead and to the right is the

**Chapter Room** where we can admire the large *Crucifixion* and below, *the Madonna and the Holy Women among the Saints and Founders of the*

*Monastic orders,* a masterpiece of Angelico's painting (1442). Under the portico is the famous bell called "la piagnona" (the crier) attributed to Donatello which, at the time of Savonarola, was in the bell-tower of the Church. It is the historic bell that called everyone to prayer on the tragic day that St. Mark's was put under seige for the arrest of Savonarola, who was called "il piagnone", because he lamented the misfortunes of the citizens due to the corrupt times, prophesying what would come about if the city was not rid of the evil undermining it.

Farther ahead to the right we enter the small *Corridor* that leads to the second cloister by Michelozzo (closed to the public because it is the property of the monks). Through the glass door we can observe this *second cloister* and the modern rooms of the first floor where the Dominican friars live. Guido Carocci collected, in this cloister, many architectural fragments originally in the old center of the city. The beautiful staircase on the right leads to the

**First Floor.** From the beautiful ceiling to the small cells, it is conserved in its original structure, that reminds us of the times and the stark living quarters of famous Dominicans. On the wall at the head of the stairs, the famous *Annunciation* by Beato Angelico (fig. 102), against a Renaissance portico background: Moving along the left corridor, we point out that the frescoes in the cells on the right are by followers of Angelico, while those on the left are, for the most part, by the master himself. They represent; in the first cell, *Noli me tangere;* third cell, *Annunciation* of a light and simple composition; sixth cell, *Transfiguration;* ninth cell, *Incoronation.* Walking down the entire length of the corridor, at the end, on the right, we enter the

**Prior's Quarter.** This consists of a vestibule and two small cells and was where Savonarola lived. In the vestibule are two pantings by Fra Bartolomeo representing: *Portrait of Savonarola* and *St. Peter Martyr* in the semblance of Savonarola. The *Execution of Savonarola in Signoria Square* is a copy from an old print. The small marble monument by Duprè (1873) shows *Savonarola before the Magistrates.* The study room contains, remains of a tunic, a rosary and other objects belonging to Savonarola. In the bedroom, *Crucifix* in the style of Angelico that, it is believed, Savanarola used when he preached in the Florentine squares after his excommunication. The rooms, severe and suggestive, bring to mind Florence divided into "piagnoni" and "arrabbiati" (criers and the angry), and Savonarola's personality, still much discussed. Walking towards the exit, the left hand cells have frescoes of *St. Dominic at the foot of the Cross* by Angeliso's helpers.

On the wall halfway down the corridor: *Madonna and Saints* by Angelico and helpers. Returning to the entrance, observe on the right wall,

Fig. 102 - St. Mark's Museum - Angelico: Annunciation

the *Crucifix* with *St. Dominic praying* by Angelico. Continuing on the left, cell no. 31 (at the head of the stairs) where St. Antonino lived, containing the *geneological tree of the Dominicans, death mask,* and other sacred objects belonging to the Saint.

Next is the double cell no. 32 where Angelico is said to have lived, altered later with frescoes attributed to the master. Farther ahead, from the large window, a splendid view of the courtyard. Among the frescoes that can be admired in the small cells that follow are: in cell no. 34, *Prayer in the Garden;* in cell no. 35, the *Communion of the Apostles in the presence of the Virgin* by Angelico. On the right of the corridor, cells 38 and 39 were reserved for Cosimo the Elder, when he would leave his palace and retire here to meditate. In the first, that served as a vestibule, *Crucifixion* from the school of Gozzoli; in the second, *bust of St. Antonino, portrait of Cosimo the Elder* and, on the front wall, the *Epiphany,* with the personages thought to be those seen by Angelico during the Council of Florence of 1439 which took place under Cosimo's patronage. Returning towards the exit, on the left, opposite to the large window, we enter the splendid

**Library.** A vast rectangular room, divided into aisles by small, slim columns (1441), where Michelozzo created the prototype of the Renaissance library, but at the same time stayed within the range of the monastic tradition. In the cases are valuable liturgical manuscripts of the XIV and XV centuries. At the entrance to the library, we observe on the wall, the epigraph that commemorates the place where Savonarola was arrested on April 8, 1498.

Heading towards the exit, at the bottom of the stairs, on the right is the **Small Refectory**, where Domenico Ghirlandaio (c. 1483) frescoed the *Last Supper* that he repeated, with variations, in the Convent of Ognissanti. On the walls, valuable "Della Robbia's".

Leaving the Museum and looking at the large wall on Via Cavour, that encloses the garden (today belonging to the Officers' Club) we see the plaque that marks the place where the "Old Academy of St. Mark" was held, in which Michelangelo in contrast with his father's wishes made his first passes in sculpture, encouraged and helped by Lorenzo the Magnificent. At the end of the wall on the right is the imposing construction by Buontalenti (1574), called "Casino of St. Mark", now the Court of Appeals. On the right of the Museum, on Via Lamarmora, is the Administration Building of the University of Florence. At the beginning of Via Ricasoli is the graceful XIV cent. loggia restored in 1935, that was once a part of the old hospital of S. Matteo, now seat of the Academy of Fine Arts. Farther ahead, at no. 60 Via Ricasoli, is the entrance to the Gallery of the Academy and Tribune of David.

Fig. 103

# GALLERY OF THE ACADEMY AND TRIBUNE OF DAVID

From the vestibule we enter the first room with the original plaster model by Giambologna for the marble sculptures of the *Rape of the Sabines* (in Piazza Signoria), and various works by mannerists of the XVI Century. Then from here to the large rooom (fig. 103) where we can admire the *Prisoners* which leads us triumphantly up to the celebrated David (fig. 104) by Michelangelo (height of the statue 4,10 meters, base 2 meters). This was sculpted by the artist between 1501 and 1505, when he was about 25 years old. It is a symbolic statue which had been placed in front of the Signoria Palace, as the guardian of the Liberty of the Florentine Republic, and was moved here in 1873, having been replaced in Signoria Square by a copy. The heroic figure of a young athlete, sculpted during one of Michelangelo's most serene moments, is shown in the act of vigilant expectation, his body showing vibrant tension, determined to win or die. On the stand to the right of the David, *bronze bust of Michelangelo,* by his pupil and friend Daniele da Volterra. On the walls of the Gallery are splendid and priceless Flemish tapestries with *Stories from Genesis,* following cartoons by the Flemish painter Van Orley (1552). Below, we can admire the celebrated *Prisoners* who seem to fight with the material that envelops them in order to emerge plastically. These famous statues were conceived for the tomb of Pope Julius II, but were made smaller than originally planned.

Between these Prisoners on the right, is the *St. Matthew,* a statue destined for the Cathedral, together with a series of Apostles. In this incomplete work, Michelangelo surpasses classical art, showing, with great vigor, his philosophical and dramatic concept of the "idea enclosed in the marble", to be liberated "little by little". Farther ahead, on the right is a *Pietà* called the *Palestrina Pietà* because it came from Palestrina near Rome, when it was given to the Gallery by the State in 1940 (fig. 105). Some critics believe it to be by his followers since it does not have the drammatic force as found in the "Pietà" in the Cathedral.

Before Michelangelo's Pietà, on the left we enter the remodelled rooms, in which, at the entrance we can admire the famous *Cassone* or marriage chest, by an unknown Florentine of the XV cent., improperly called the *Wedding Procession of the Adimari* interesting for its artistic value and for its portraits of Florentines shown in the typical costumes and hair styles of the era, in S. Giovanni Square. In the next rooms, among the most important works: graceful *Madonna and Child* attributed to Botticelli. Also shown are other works by Florentine

**Fig. 104** - Gallery of the Academy and Tribune of David

**Fig. 105 - Michelangelo: Palestrina Pietà**

artists and by Perugino.

At the end of the left wing of the Tribune is a room containing numerous busts and plaster models for sculptures of nineteenth century Tuscan artists. Towards the exit, there are three rooms containing historic works selected from those of the XIII and XIV Centuries; (Figs.106) the most notable being the *Magdalen* of the "Magdalen's Master", Giovanni da Milano's *Pietà* (1365) and the *Stories of St. Francis and of Christ*, by Taddeo Gaddi. Before the vestibule, the staircase leads to a room containing a rich collection of the works of Byzantine and Florentine painters of the end of the XIV Century and the first half of the XV Century. Leaving the Gallery and turning to the left we arrive at

**Fig. 106 - Room of plaster casts**

the nearby Square of the Belle Arti where, at no.80 Via degli Alfani, you can visit the small but important Museum of musical instruments of the **Luigi Cherubini conservatory**. (closed for repair).

Farther ahead, at no. 78, entrance to the

**Museum of Pietre dure or Mosaics** the only one if its kind, begun by Duke Ferdinand I Medici (1588). This "workshop" that enriched the Chapel of the Princes in St. Lorenzo with its rare stones originating from all parts of the world furnishes material of an elevated decorative value to churches, palaces and museums in Florence, Italy and the world.

# THIRD ITINERARY

*Piazza della Repubblica - Straw Market - Via por Santa Maria - Ponte Vecchio - Pitti Palace: Palatine Gallery, Royal Apartments, Museum of Silverware, Boboli Gardens, Gallery of Modern Art, Museum of Antique Coaches - Church of S. Spirito - Church of the Carmine.*
(This itinerary is indicated by numbers 11, 12, 13, 14, 15 and 16 on our monumental map)

## PIAZZA DELLA REPUBBLICA (Republic Square)

Formerly Piazza Vittorio Emanuele II. In order to build this square the Old Market, economic hearth of Old Florence (1895), was destroyed, as can be read above the large, overpowering arch. On the left is the portico of the Central Post Office, by Sabatini and Vagnetti (1917). This Square is a popular meeting place for Florentines and turists because of its many cafès.
In front of the hotel Savoy, on a tall column, is a reproduction of the statue of *Abundance,* that was here at the time of the "Old Market". To the right of the "Upim" department store, the short and elegant Via Calimala leads to the well known *Straw market* (new market) with the Loggia by Giovanni Battista del Tasso (1547-51). The famous "wild boar" (fig. 107), called "il Porcellino" (the little pig), by Tacca (1612, restored), is a copy of a classical marble statue currently in the Uffizi Gallery. At one time the Banking Center, (mentioned in the introduction) was found here. In the center of the Loggia is a small round slab, upon which the bankrupts were effectively punished. Por Santa Maria (with its buildings reconstructed from the ruins of the last war) partly conserves its medieval character because of a few "Tower-houses" especially those on Via delle Terme and Borgo SS. Apostoli, on the right. On the left, the *Square and the Church of SS. Stefano and Cecilia,* originally built in 1116, worked over later, and, having been destroyed in 1944 by German mines, has been restored to its original aspect.
Farther ahead is the Ponte Vecchio.

**Ponte Vecchio** (fig. 108), attributed to Neri di Fioravanti (1348), who replaced an old wooden bridge destroyed by the flood of 1333 (it was damaged in 1944 by the retreating Germans and by the flood of Nov. 4, 1966). The Ponte Vecchio (Old Bridge), with its small characteristic shops, is known throughout the world as the jewellers' bridge; formerly

Fig. 107

**Fig. 108 - Ponte Vecchio (Old Bridge)**

there were butcher shops. On the terrace is a square-based monument surmounted by a bust of *Cellini* by Romanelli (1900). Above the shops, on the left hand side, is the "Vasarian Corridor" that joins the Uffizi Gallery to the Pitti Palace. After the Ponte Vecchio begins Via Guicciardini, rebuilt after the war. Farther ahead on the left, under the Vasarian corridor, is the *Square and Church of S. Felicita* (XI cent.), erected on an old cemetery, worked over in the following centuries. Under the portico of the Church, on the right, among other works, is the *Tomb of Cardinal de' Rossi* by Raffaele da Montelupo, brought here in 1736. In the interior we can admire the famous *Deposition* by Pontormo, in the first chapel on the right. The Capponi Chapel that Brunelleschi built for the Barbadori family was later altered by Ruggeri during the remodelling of the church. The upper balcony was used by the Grand Dukes of Lorraine when they came here from the Pitti Palace for their religious services. Continuing along Via Guicciardini, at no. 18 is a plaque marking the house in which Machiavelli lived. Ahead on the left is the *Guicciardini Palace* with its beautiful garden, attributed to Baccio d'Agnolo. Here the historian Guicciardini was born.

We then reach the vast square dominated by the imposing Pitti Palace.

Fig. 109 - Pitti Palace

## PITTI PALACE

The Palace is built of ashlar (fig. 109), inspired by ancient Roman construction. It was begun by Luca Fancelli (1458), following a design by Brunelleschi, to satisfy the great ambitions of the influential banker Luca Pitti, one time friend and follower of the Medici, who, jealous of their power, plotted against Piero the "gouty". The conspiracy was discovered thanks to the careful surveillance of his young son Lorenzo (later the Magnificent).

Luca Pitti, ruined by his banking speculations, left the Palace inconplete. Later in 1540, Cosimo I (with the dowry brought by his wife Eleanor of Toledo) bought it from Bonaccorso, Luca's great grandson.

Cosimo I moved here from Palazzo Vecchio and ordered Vasari to join the two palaces with the corridor that runs over the Ponte Vecchio. Eleanor of Toledo commissioned Tribolo to transform the hillside called "Boboli" into the famous "Boboli Gardens" that scenically enclose the palace. The original building consisted of three doors alternated by four windows on the ground floor, seven windows on the upper floors

**Figs. 110-111 - Valerio Cioli: Dwarf Morgante - Buontalenti: Grotto**

and was crowned with a panoramic loggia. Ammannati, better known as an architect than as a sculptor (1558), without altering Brunelleschi's plan, closed two doors substituting them with windows, lengthened the façade and created the most beautiful courtyard of the Renaissance on the interior. Later Giulio and Alfonso Parigi (1620) further lengthened the façade, adding three windows on each side. Between 1764-1819 Giuseppe Ruggeri added the so-called "rondò", the beautiful lateral portico which juts out onto the square. When the Medici died out, the Palace became the home of the Lorraines, who were driven out in 1859. During the period when Florence was the capital of Italy (1865-71), the Palace housed the Savoy court. After 1871, it was the private home of the royal family. With the advent of the Republic (1946), the great Palace and all its art treasures, became the property of the State.

On the left of the façade, from the gate called of "Bacchus" because of the grotesque fountain (fig. 110) by Valerio Cione, representing Morgante the dwarf riding a tortoise, one can reach the Grotto of Buontalenti (fig. 111) and from here the Boboli Gardens mentioned later. See above the already mentioned Vasari's Corridor, reopened to the public in 1973, full of works and selfportraits of famous artists.

**BOBOLI**

**GARDEN**

**PITTI SQUARE**

**ENTRY**

ROYAL APARTMENTS

1-2 Vestibule
3 Gallery of the statues
4 Dining Hall (or of the niches)
5 Green Hall
6 Hall of the Throne
7 Blue Hall
8 Chapel
9 Hall of the parrots
10 Yellow Hall
11 The Queen's Bedroom
12 The King's Bedroom
13 Study
14 Sitting room
15 Antechamber
16 Hall of Bona
17 Dancing Hall (or White Hall)

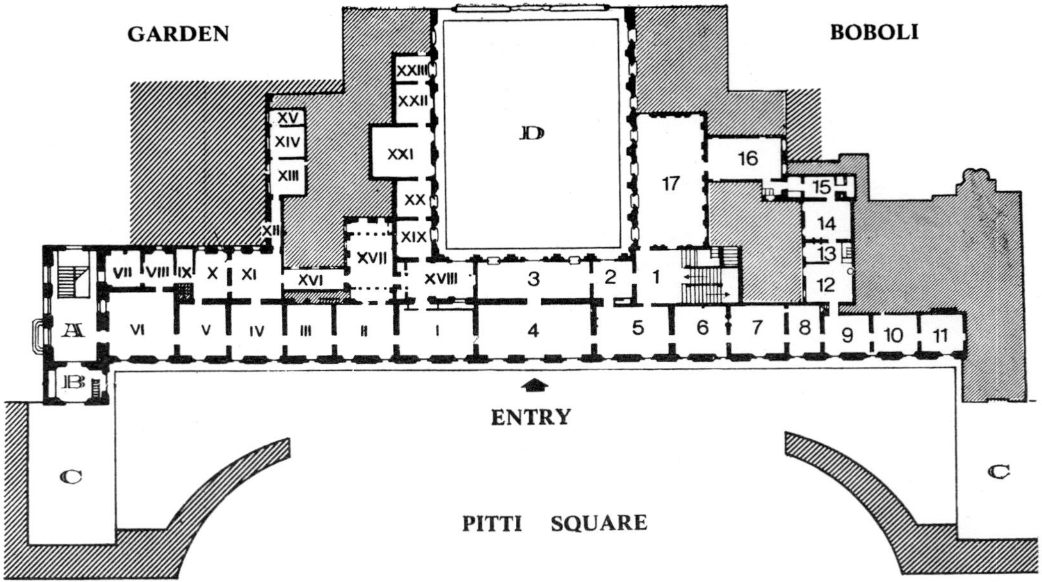

**PITTI PALACE**
**PALATINA GALLERY**
**1st Floor**

| | | | |
|---|---|---|---|
| I | Hall of Venus | XIV | Hall of Flora |
| II | Hall of Apollo | XV | Hall of Putti |
| III | Hall of Mars | XVI | Hall of Poccetti |
| IV | Hall of Jupiter | XVII | Hall of music |
| V | Hall of Saturn | | |
| VI | Hall of the Iliad | | |
| VII | Hall of the Stove | | |
| VIII | Hall of the Education of Jupiter | | |
| IX | Bath | XVIII | Hall of Castagnoli |
| X | Hall of Ulysses | XIX-XXIII | Quarter of Volterrano |
| XI | Hall of Promotheus | XXIV-XXVIII | Halls closed to the Public |
| XII | Corridor of the columns | | |
| XIII | Hall of Justice | | |

A. Vestibule
B. Hall of the Cup
C. Terrace
D. Ammannati's Court-yard

Fig. 112 - Palatine Gallery: Iliad Room

Figs. 113-114 - Sustermans: Portrait of Prince Waldermar of Denmark - Raphael: Madonna of the Grand duke

# PALATINE GALLERY

(Closed, save changes, every Monday. For hours see "Information" section).
One reaches the Gallery from the main staircase of the palace, built by Ammannati on the right corner of the arcade looking on to the courtyard.

**Palatine Gallery,** which was begun by Cosimo II (1620). The vast collection has continuously enriched by his successors. Because of the marriage of Anna Maria Ludovica Medici and John William, the Elector Palatine, the museum was called "Palatine Gallery". In 1820 the museum was opened to the public by the Lorraines (successors of the Medici), and in 1911, it was ceded to the State by Vittorio Emanuele III. The vision that the Gallery offers is splendid, especially on the days when the "Royal Apartments" are opened and the perspective effect of these sumptous rooms is lengthened.
Here the works of art are not placed in chronological order as in the Uffizi Gallery, but rather displayed with an essentially decorative taste according to the spirit of the princely courts. It is a picture gallery. To facilitate the visit we have included a practical plan. We mention that the works not cited can be easily identified by reading their relative plates.

**Room I. Of Venus.** Here ends the series of splendid rooms built for Cosimo II, the initiator of this Gallery. In the vault frescoed by Pietro da Cortona and Ciro Ferri (1641-42) we see *"La Bella"* restored) and the *Portrait of Pietro Aretino.* Between these two paintings is vain held back by Eros), directing him toward Hercules. The stuccoes representing various Medici personalities, are by Roman artists. Moving from left to right, by Titian we see *"la bella"* (restored) and the *Portrait of Pietro Aretino.* Between these two paintings is the *Sacred Conversation* by Pitati. Above, a large *Seascape* by the Neapolitan Salvator Rosa, who also painted the one on the opposite wall. At the beginning and at the end of the next wall are two very rare *Landscapes* by Rubens: *Return of the Peasants from the Fields* (fig. 125) and *Ulysses on the Islands of the Feaci.* On the far wall: *Portrait of Julius II,* a copy by Titian of an original by Raphael (now lost). Next is the celebrated *Concert* (fig. 126), once attributed to Giorgione, now believed to be a young work by Titian.
In the centre of the room is the *Venere Italica,* by Canova whose model for the work was Paolina Borghese, sister of Napoleon and wife of Prince Borghese.
From this room we enter the sumptous *Royal Apartments.*

**Room II. Of Apollo.** Its name derives from the subject of the ceiling, by Pietro da Cortona and Ciro Ferri (1642-46), who decorated it with white and colored stuccoes and Medici crests. In the center of the vault, the *Glorification of Cosimo I,* shown in the figure of the *young man,* whom *Virtue and Glory* lead to *Apollo* in the presence of Hercules, Nymphs and Atlantis. On the wall near the window is the famous and exuberant *Mary Magdalen* (fig. 123), a typical female representation by Titian with its warm and golden color. Also by Titian we can admire, on the right of the door, the celebrated *Portrait of the Gentleman with the Grey Eyes,* considered one of the most important portraits by Titian and Italian art. Above is the ample *Depositian* by Andrea del Sarto. On the following walls: *Madonna and Saints,* by Rosso Fiorentino, one of the major works of this mannerist painter whose figures are tormented and whose color is vivid and fiery; *Holy Family* by Andrea del Sarto, rendered with classical equilibrium; *Cleopatra* by Guido Reni, placed here temporarily. On the wall near the window: *Portraits of Charles I of England and Henriette of France,* daughter of Maria dei Medici (restored work, believed by some to be of the Van Dyck school).

**Room III. Of Mars.** On the ceiling, Allegory of Mars by Pietro da Cortona and Ciro Ferri (1645-47). Moving from left to right, two beautiful *Madonnas and Child,* by Murillo (fig. 121). Between these two, *the Four Philosophers,* by Rubens (fig. 122), who portrayed himself in the figure standing on the left. Seated next to him is his *brother Philip,* humanist and philosopher, followed by the distinguished philosopher Justus Lipsius, who seems to be explaining a passage from Seneca, and his pupil Jan Wouver (restored work). Followed by a *Portrait of a Man* by Veronese and the large *Consequences of War,* by Rubens (1638),

Fig. 115

Figs. 116-117 - Raphael: Portraits of Angelo and Maddalena Doni
Fig. 118 - Palatine Gallery - Room of Jupiter

alluding to the thirty-years war that devastated a great part of Europe. Next is Titian's *Portrait of Cardinal Ippolito dei Medici* in a Hungarian costume. Next is the famous *Portrait of Cardinal Bentivoglio* by Van Dyck from Antwerp (1559-1640), a deeply psychological interpretation rendered with elegance and simplicity. Finally, by Tintoretto, *Portrait of Luigi Cornaro,* author.

**Room IV. Of Jupiter** (fig. 118). The ceiling by Pietro da Cortona and Ciro Ferri (1643-46) representing the *Allegory of Jupiter* with reference to the glories of Cosimo I. In the center of the room is the awkward and mediocre *Victory* by Consano (1867), that should be removed in order to allow us to admire the many important works of art. From left to right: *young St. John the Baptist* (restored) by Andrea del Sarto (fig. 119). Followed by the *Deposition* by Fra' Bartolomeo, with its pyramidal composition. Above, *Nymphs attacked by the Satyrs* by Rubens. Followed by the *Portrait of Guidobaldo della Rovere,* by Bronzino, and the grandiose figure of *St. Mark* by Fra' Bartolomeo, who was inspired by Michelangelo's prophets. Above the door, the *Annunciation* by Andrea del Sarto and the *Assumption,* left incomplete because of the artist's death. On the next wall, *Battle Scene* by the French artist Jacques Courtois, called il Borgognone. Near the door is the famous *Fornarina* (baker's daughter) by Raphael (fig. 120), a magnificent portrait rendered with the warmth of Venetian color, known as *the Veiled Lady.* The beautiful Roman brunette is the same one that the artist idealized in the Madonna of the Chair. Near the window: *Three Ages of Man,* school of Giorgione of the early XVI cent. On the opposite wall, *Madonna del Sacco* by Perugino (restored). Against the walls are valuable *tables* made with Florentine mosaics.

**Room V. Of Saturn** with the ceiling representing the *Allegory of Saturn,* alluding to the virtues of Cosimo I, frescoed by Pietro da Cortona and Ciro Ferri (1663-1665). This room contains a great number of works by Raphael. Beginning from left to right we can admire: the *Madonna of the Grand Duke* (1504) by Raphael, so called because it was the favorite of the Medici Grand Dukes, inspired by Perugino and Leonardo's "sfumato". Following are the *St. Peter* by Guercino and the realistic *Portrait of a man* by Carracci. Above, the *Dispute of the Holy Trinity* by Andrea del Sarto (1517), that inspired Raphael for the same subject in the Vatican. Below is the *Portrait of Tommaso Inghirami,* by Raphael (c. 1514). Following, by the same artist are: the famous *Portraits of Agnolo and Maddalena Doni* (1506 - figs. 116-117). Between these two is the *Vision of Ezechiel* (c. 1518) showing the influence of Michelangelo. Above, *Madonna of the Baldaquin* (1506), incomplete. Next, by Perugino are the large *Deposition,* with its beautiful Umbrian landscape, and the exquisite *Mary Magdalen,* below. The solemn and monumental *Jesus and the Evangelists,* above right, is by Fra' Bartolomeo. Below, *Portrait of an Unknoewn Man,* called the *Goldsmith,* is attributed to Ridolfo del Ghirlandaio. On the following wall are: Portrait of Cardinal Dovizzi da Bibbiena, believed to be by Raphael's helpers: *St. Rose* and the graceful *St. John Sleeping* by Dolci; and finally, the famous *Madonna of the Chair* (fig. 115) by Raphael, painted in Rome (1515-16) using his beloved "Fornarina" as a model.

**Room VI. Iliad Room** (fig. 112). This room was added by the Dukes of Lorraine. In the ceiling, frescoed by Luigi Sabatelli (1819), are *Episodes* taken from the Homeric poem. In the center of the room is the statue of *Charity* by Lorenzo Bartolini (1824), rendered with profound humanity. Beginning at the left and moving towards the right: *Portrait of an unknown woman,* called *The Pregnant Lady* (Gravida) by Raphael (c. 1505), from his Florentine period. Next is the grandiose *Assumption* by Andrea del Sarto, who repeats the same subject in the large picture on the opposite wall. Further along is a *Portrait of a Woman* by Ridolfo del Ghirlandaio (son of Domenico), who was inspired by Raphael's *Gravida.*

On the following wall, among the numerous works, we mention the large canvas showing the *ecstasy of St. Philip Neri* by Maratta (XVIII cent.) of the Roman school, inspired by Guido Reni.

Near the windows, famous *Portrait of Waldemar Christian,* Prince of Denmark, by Sustermans (fig. 113) and the rare *Equestrian Portrait of Philip IV of Spain,* by Velasques (restored).

Figs. 119-120 - Room of Jupiter - A. Del Sarto: St. John - Raphael: the Veiled Lady
Figs. 121-122 - Room of Mars - Murillo: Madonna and Child - Rubens: Four Philosophers

# ROYAL APARTMENTS

Remodelled in Empire style by the Savoy family, these rooms witnessed the most famous court receptions. (The royal family's private life evolved in the small adjoining nineteenth century palace called "La Meridiana", built by the Dukes of Lorraine, with its entrance from the Boboli Gardens behind Ammannati's courtyard joined to the "large Palace" by a internal passageway). Among the most important works in these sumptuous ex-royal Apartments we mention:

**Room 4. Of the Niches** (Dining Room). So-called because of the copies of classical statues in the niches of a purely decorative value. The neo-classic decoration is by Giuseppe Maria Terreni and Giuseppe Castagnoli. On the walls is a series of portraits of the Medici in their different costumes, by Sustermans, the court painter of the Medici family. Also here are Japanese and Sevres vases.

**Room 5. Green Room** (formerly room of the guard). Called Green room for the color of the brocade that covers the walls. The decoration is by Castagnoli while the chiaroscuro ceiling, with allegorical subjects in honor of the Medici, is by Luca Giordano. On the walls are four Gobelins tapestries with *stories of Esther,* made by Audran following cartoons by Jean François de Troy (1737-40). The large intarsia cabinet is of XVII cent.

**Room 6. Throne Room** (fig. 128). On the ceiling is Jupiter between Juno and Minerva, by Paolo Sarti, chiaroscuro decoration is by Castagnoli. Under the baldaquin is the *Throne* that served for the swearing in of the kings of Italy. On the walls are *Gobelins* from the series of *Esther,* portraits by Sustermans and François Paurbus the Younger. The furniture is in Empire style and the vases are Oriental.

**Room 7. Blue Room.** So called because of the color of the upholstery fabric. On the walls are the Gobelin tapestries showing the *Triumph of the Gods,* from cartoons by Noel Cypel. The portraits are by Sustermans and represent members of the Medici family. A Chinese vase is on the fireplace.

**Room 8. Chapel.** Decorated in the XVII cent., with partial modifications done in the neo-classic era. The *Medici portraits* are by Sustermans. Near the window is a *Madonna and Child,* by Dolci, with the frame made of cornelian. Next to it is a beautiful cabinet made of ebony, ivory and alabaster.

**Room 9. Of the Parrots.** So called because of the parrots that decorate

**Figs. 123-124 - Room of Apollo - Titian: Magdalen and the Gentleman with the grey eyes**

the brocade of the walls. The two tapestries belong to the famous series of the *Triumph of the Gods.* This room was the antechamber of Queen Margherita's Apartment, which was separate from that of King Umberto I. On the left wall: *Portrait of Giulia Varano, Duchess of Urbino* by Titian.

On the right wall, Portrait of Francesco I by Hans von Aachen. The stove is Austrian. Next are the Apartments of Queen Margherita.

### The apartments of Queen Margherita

**Room 10. Yellow room.** Decorated with yellow brocade and splendid Gobelin tapestries (1735-45) showing *hunting scenes of the court of Louis XV,* from cartoons by J.B. Oudry. The Florentine mosaic table with daisies in chalcedony intarsia was presented to the Queen by her ladies-in-waiting.

**Room 11. Bed chamber.** On the walls are four other tapestries from the series of the *Hunt of Louis XV.* Portraits are by Sustermans and by Paurbus. The furniture is in Empire style, the *Table and Kneeler* are of Florentine mosaic. Other rooms follow but unfortunately are closed to the public. Perhaps the sumptuous Queen's drawing-room will be visible with its splendid brocades inspired by Chinese art. We return to the Room of the Parrots to continue on the right in the

Figs. 125-126 - Room of Venus - Rubens: Landscape - Titian: the Concert

**Apartments of King Umberto I**
**Room 12. King's Bed chamber.** Among other works on the walls: Tapestry from the *Triumph of the Gods,* and *Medici portraits* by Sustermans. The kneeler is of semi-precious stones, the large Austrian stove decorated in stucco.

**Room 13. Study.** Enriched with brocades, mirrors, lamps and a *Portrait of Claudia dei Medici* by Sustermans.

**Room 14. Drawing room.** A particularly interesting work is the Tapestry of the series of the Hunt of Louis XV.

**Room. 15. Ante-chamber.** On the walls are four small XVI cent. Florentine tapestries by Giovanni Roost, from cartoons by Bronzino. On the table is a marble bust representing a *young portrait of Queen Margherita* by Pagliaccetti (1869); followed by a small landscape with a view the Boboli Gardens. Through the corridor on the left we enter

**The Room of Bona 16.** It was entirely frescoed by Poccetti, who represented, on the walls: 1) Defeat of the city of Bona in Africa 2) Defeat of Prevesa in Albania 3) Silvio Piccolomini announces the taking of Bona to Cosimo II; 4) View of the Port of Leghorn; in the vault, *Apotheosis of Cosimo I.* Observe the two large and valuable chandeliers from Bohemia.

**Room 17. Ball-room**, (fig. 127) called the *White Room* because of the stuccoes that decorate it. The architecture is by Gaspare Maria Paoletti (XVIII cent.), the stupendous stucco decoration by the Albertolli brothers of Lugano (1776-80). On the door are two Faunas by Innocenzo Spinazzi. This room with its beautiful *chandeliers from Murano,* that at the time of the Savoy was used for grand balls, is now used for concerts. For the exit, we continue on in the Gallery passing through rooms 1, 2 and 3 containing antique statues and Medicean tapestries with episodes about the family. From the windows we can enjoy splendid views of the Boboli Gardens and the Belvedere Fortress. Farther ahead,

**Room VII. Of the Stove** (last room of the Gallery). So called because of the large stove that was found here. The walls, frescoed by Pietro da Cortona (1637-40) represent the *Four Ages of the Earth:* Gold, Silver, Bronze and Iron. On the ceiling the Cardinal Virtues and the Great Kingdoms are by Matteo Rosselli (1622). On the floor, the *Triumph of Bacchus* in ceramic (damaged from wear), the work of Benedetto Bocchi (1640).

**Room VIII. Of Jupiter,** from the ceiling subject, frescoed by Luigi Cata-

Fig. 127 - White room (Royal Apartments)
Fig. 128 - Throne Room (Royal Apartments)

143

ni 1819). Here are displayed: a *Caricature on Copper* by Callot, *Judith with the Head of Holofernes* by Allori, and the famous *Sleeping Cupid* (fig. 133) by Caravaggio, rendered with luminous plasticity.

**Room IX, Bathroom**, in Empire style, work of Cacialli (XIX cent.).
**Room X. Of Ulysses** (see plan). The name of the room derives from the ceiling fresco by Martellini (XIX cent.), with Stories of Ulysses. The fresco symbolizes the return of the Lorraines to Florence after the Napoleonic invasions. Among the works are: *Mary Magdalen* by Dolci; the *Madonna dell'Impannata* (because of the window motif) by Raphael and helpers; *Ecce Homo* by Cigoli and a *Portrait of Andrea Frisier* by Tintoretto. On the wall (perhaps temporarily) is the gracious *Bacchus* (fig. 131) by Reni, inspired by Caravaggio. Farther ahead in the small corridor is

**Room XI. Of Prometheus.** So named because of the subject of the ceiling by Collignon (1830). Among the most notable works in the room is the large tondo (fig. 132) by Fra Filippo Lippi, Botticelli's teacher, representing *the Madonna and Child, Meeting of St. Anna and Joachim at the Golden Gate and the Birth of the Virgin.* Below, the delicate *Dance of Apollo with the Nine Muses* is by Giulio Romano, pupil of Raphael. On the right (see plan) follow:

**Corridor XII of the Columns:** here are graceful works of the Dutch and Flemish schools including *Orpheus in Hell* by Breughel and, at the end, a *Portrait of Maria Ludovica with her Husband,* the Elector Palatine by Douven. Also observe other interesting works identified by their relative plates.

**Room XIII. Of Justice** takes its name from the allegorical fresco of the ceiling, by Fedi (1830). On the walls, *The Saviour* and the *Portrait of Tommaso Mosti,* by Titian (both restored). *Portraits of a Gentleman and Lady,* by Moroni; works by Tintoretto, Bassano Veronese and others. On the easel is a realistic *Portrait of Anna Maria Ludovica,* the last Medici, by Douven.

**Room XIV. Of Flora.** Named for the subject of the ceiling, by Marini (1839). On the walls: famous *Stories of Joseph,* by Andrea del Sarto, *Martyrdom of St. Agatha,* by the Venetian painter Sebastiano del Piombo, and *portraits* by Bronzino.

**Room XV. Of the Putti.** So called because of the ceiling subject, also by Marini. In this room are works of Flemish and Dutch artists. Among these are: *Girl with a Candle,* by Schalcken; *the Three Graces,* by Rubens; *Hunting Scenes, Seascapes, Flowers and Fruit* by Rachel Ruysch.

144

**Fig. 129 - View of the Amphitheater in the Boboli Gardens**

From the window is a splendid view of the city with the Palazzo Vecchio and, in the background, the hills of Fiesole.

**Room XVI. Of Poccetti,** who, in 1620, decorated the ceiling with the Triumphs of Ferdinand I of the Medici. Among the most important works, on the wall near the door, is the realistic Martyrdom of St. Bartholomew, by Ribera nicknamed "lo Spagnoletto". whose painting shows clear Caravaggesque derivation. Against the wall is a Florentine mosaic table.

**Room XVII. Music Room** (see plan). Called also room of the drums because of the tables against the walls, made in the form of drums. On the ceiling is the *Liberation of Vienna from the Turks* (1638), vast chiaroscuro fresco by Luigi Ademollo (1819), with a search for optical effects.
In the center is the large Russian malachite table on a gilded bronze base by Pierre Thomire (1819).

**Room XVIII. Castagnoli Hall** (see plan). From the name of the artist who decorated the room in chiaroscuro (1754-1832). In the center is a rich mosaic table (1815) representing, on the top, the *Triumph of Apollo* and the nine muses and, on the base, the *Four Seasons* in bronze by Duprè. The famous St. Sebastian, on the easel, a superb masculine idealization inserted into a vast, splendid Leonardesque landscape, is

**Figs. 130-131 - The Volterrano Apartments - Zocchi: Young Michelangelo - Reni: Bacchus**

the work of the Vercelli painter Antonio Bazzi called "The Sodoma" (1525), who was active in Siena where he painted this *Standard* for the *Company of St. Rocco* with, on the back, *The Virgin, St. Rocco and other Saints.* (From the window is a view of Ammannati's Courtyard (fig. 129) and the Amphitheater in the Boboli Gardens.

**Room XIX-XXIII. Apartments of Volterrano**, so-called because of the artist Franceschini da Volterra (XVIII century), who decorated the ceiling of the first room with Allegories. On the walls are works by the same artist and Giovanni da San Giovanni. In the center of the room is a statue of *Michelangelo as a Young Boy Sculpting the Mask of a Faun* (fig. 130) by Zocchi (XIX cent.)

**Room II. Of Volterrano.** Among the XVII cent. works we point out the painting of *Mary Magdalen* and *St. Francis in Adoration* against the solitary cliffs of the Verna landscape, by Cigoli.

**Room of Hercules.** On the walls, the *Labors of Hercules;* on the ceiling, *Hercules Received on Olympus,* frescoes of large proportions painted by Pietro Benvenuti (1829).
Among the XVIII cent. works we point out: the realistic *Wild Boar*

Fig. 132

*Hunt,* by Snyders; *Adam and Eve,* by Furini and *Narcissus* by Curradi. In the center of the room is a magnificent Sévres Vase that Napoleon gave to Duke Ferdinand III of Lorraine. The last rooms have small interesting works by Salvator Rosa.

The classical entrance, the monumental staircase which leads to the first floor and its beautiful vestibule with a magnificent carved ceiling, were built during the Savoy reign, by Luigi del Moro (1897). In the center of the vestibule is a gracious fountain by Tribolo, sculptor and architect of the Boboli Gardens. On the easal is the famous *St. Sebastian,* a superb idealization of a man placed in the vast and splendid Leonardesque landscape, work of Antonio Bazzi called "il Sodoma" from Vercelli (1525).

If open, pass into the second *Vestibule,* with its enormous porphyry basin, where, on the left, begins Vasari's corridor. Farther ahead we go out onto the *vast terrace* with its splendid view of the Palace and the city.

## THE MUSEUM OF SILVERWARE

The entrance is in the courtyard, on the left. From the vestibule, with Medici portraits (note the portrait of Giovanna of Austria, first wife of Francesco I, the second Grand Duke, with the Pitti Palace as it was in the XVI Century, seen through the window), one goes to the rooms of the summer apartment of the grand Dukes.

**Room 1.** The largest, entirely frescoed by Giovanni da San Giovanni and by Furini (1635) to glorify the Medici. The large scenes on the walls celebrate the figure of Lorenzo the Magnificent: muses, poets, philosophers expelled from Greece at the arrival of Mahomet, find a welcome at the Court of Lorenzo represented with his circle of artists, as patron and pacifier of Italy.

From here one passes to the Treasure Room, containing precious vases in amethyst, jasper, oriental sardonyx of various ancient provenances; some with mountings of the time with Medicean symbols and the inscription LAUR.MED., indicating the collection of Lorenzo the Magnificent.

Returning to the first room, after the small private chapel which has a bronze crucifix of the Giambologna school and a prie-dieu from the hard stone Workshops, one passes on to three rooms entirely frescoed by Bologna artists Colonna and Mitelli (1640) who sought particular optical and scenographic effects. The first contains the *Cabinet of Alemagna,* in which are preserved holy vestments, used (it is believed) by Cardinal Leopold to celebrate Mass. On the walls are some sumptuous panels of Florentine mosaic. In the second room, works in mosaic and inlay from the granducal workshops. In the third room, a magnificent ebony cabinet with incrustations in relief and a statuette of the Elector Palatine Giovanni Guglielmo, husband of the Last of the Medici; in the centre is a Group of Cherubs by Bernini.

Leaving these rooms, which make up the official apartment of representation (public and private audiences, etc), one proceeds to the private apartment, which faces the interior.

**Room 1.** This was originally a bedroom: the showcases on the left side of the window contain vases, goblets, various plates and dishes in rock crystal, jasper and lapis lazuli. A rock crystal cup with lid in enamelled gold, with the initials H and D entwined of Henry II and Diana of Poitiers, and the half moon, Diana's crest, in the centre of the lid. The next showcase contains a vase in lapislazuli in the shape of an urn, designed by Buontalenti for Francis I de' Medici, with enamelled gold mounting by Jaques Bilivert (1583), of most elegant working; salt cellars and goblets in lapislazuli to designs by Buontalenti.

In the following rooms on the ground floor, there are precious works in amber and ivory, most of them German, of exceptional fineness and difficulty of execution.

A narrow staircase leads to the Mezzanine which contains the treasure of the Medici family.

In the rooms on the right: showcases containing inlays and cammeos, a rich collection of rings with antique and Renaissance settings, a large onyx cammeo of Cosimo I and his family, by Antonio de' Rossi (1557-1562); the case against the wall in the second room contains jewels which belonged to the Electrix Palatine, the last of the Medici, among which are the curious Baroque pearls mounted in gold to represent imaginary animals.

The rooms on the left. The first three house the treasure of the Bishops of Salzburg, carried away arbitrarily by the Lorraines and returned by Austria with the Treaty of San Germano. To mention a few of the works of art: cups made of ostrich egg, coconut, set in gilded silver, Medieval. A portable altar of the XVIII Century, in silver and mother-of-pearl; Mysteries of the Rosary, engravings from prints by Stradano: Madonna and Child, on silver.

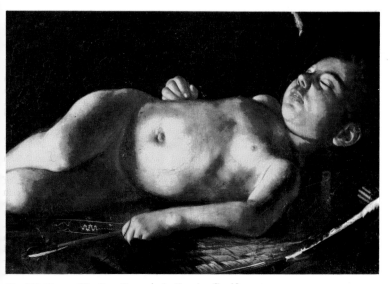

Fig. 133 - Room of Jupiter - Caravaggio: **Sleeping Cupid**

149

**Fig. 134 - Boboli Gardens: "Viottolone" (Broad Walk)**

The second room on the left contains the magnificent table service in silver, gilded and chiselled, with allegorical figures and biblical episodes (silversmiths of Augusta, 1585-90). Set apart is a service in pure gold including a flask and four cups with grotesque decorations, and enamel work with mining scenes.

One passes from the small loggia with decorations in the style of Poccetti, which runs around the Courtyard of Fame, to the last room where exotic and curious objects are shown. Next to the entrance, a showcase contains precolombian objects of art which came from the modern Mexico; and a mitre and infula embroidered with peacock feathers, a local work of art, given by Charles V to Clement VII.

In the showcase on the left: a collection of the ten emperors' heads (from Roman Commanders' batons); curious and grotesque personages, in the manner of Buontalenti.

In the right hand showcase, note the Chinese cups made from Nautilus shells and the engravings on mother-of-pearl.

# BOBOLI GARDENS

The garden rose on the hillside of Boboli at the request of Eleonora, wife of Cosimo I. It is a vast and splendid Italian style park-garden, that reflects, in every way, the taste of the high Renaissance period (masses of trees treated as architecture, lawns, grottos, fountains, etc.).

Begun by Tribolo (1550), it was continued by Ammannati, Buontalenti and Alfonso Parigi. Entering through the *Bacchus Gateway,* at the end of the short walk is the splendid *Grotto of Buontalenti* (1583). In the third grotto is the beautiful *Venus* by Giambologna. "The prisoners" on the sides of the first *grotto* are copies of Michelangelo's originals in the "Academy". Continuing on the right of the garden, the avenue which curves up to the right leads to the large *Amphitheater* built by the Medici in the XVII century. In the center, the large granite *basin* comes from the Baths of Caracalla. Even the Egyptian Obelisk, reduced in proportion, comes from Rome. From here we can admire the courtyard of the Pitti Palace closed by *the Fountain* called *"of the Artichoke"* the work of Tadda and Susini (XVII cent.). On the side the Palace is the gracious XIX century 'little Palace' called *"La Meridiana"* constructed by Paoletti and Poccianti, ex-private residence of the Savoy. From here is a splendid view of the city and the hills of Fiesole.

Moving up from the Amphitheater we come to the Neptune Pond with the *Bronze Statue* by Lorenzi (1565). Still higher we enter, if open, the *Garden of the Cavaliere,* with the small house and panoramic garden that was the summer residence of Giangastone, the last Medici Grand Duke. Returning to the Neptune Pond, farther ahead to the right we come to the vast space with the magnificent *cedars of Lebanon.* From here begins the "Viottolone" (fig. 134) (large lane), flanked by high cypresses, pines, statues and other small lateral walks, that leads down to the vast and picturesque "Isolotto" (fig. 136) (small island), with the *statue of Ocean* (from an original by Giambologna in the Bargello), and three statues on the base symbolizing the great rivers: *Nile, Euphrates* and *Ganges.*

Fig. 135 - Palatine Gallery - Museum of Silverware - Room IV

Fig. 136 - Boboli Gardens - L'Isolotto, Ocean (detail)

# GALLERY OF MODERN ART

The entrance is through the central door of the Pitti Palace. The Gallery is located in the numerous vast rooms of the second floor (one time home of the Lorraines), and offers a splendid panoramic view of the city. This important Gallery, founded by the Provisional Government in 1860, was enriched with works belonging to the city galleries, with the group of "Macchiaioli" paintings from the Diego Martelli collection, and with gifts from collectors of modern art. The large collection allows us to admire a rather complete panorama of Italian painting and sculpture from the XIX century to modern times.

Among the artists represented are: Pietro Benvenuti, Canova, Bartolini, Dupré, Ciseri, Bezzuoli, Ussi, Induno, Palizzi, Michetti, Morselli, Mancini, Achille D'Orsi, Trentacoste, Fattori (fig. 138 bis), Lega, Abate, Signorini, Cabianca, Boldini, Medardo Rosso, Sironi, Spadini, Carena, De Chirico (fig. 138) and many others. Among the non-Italians are: Lumbrach, Scheffer, Sargent, Durant.

The Gallery is continuously enriched by generous gifts and new acquisitions.

Fig. 137 - Baldassarre Franceschini: A joke of the Parson Arlotto

Fig. 138 - Giorgio De Chirico: Still Life

►

Fig. 138 bis - Fattori: Cart pulled by Oxen

Fig. 138 bis

## PIAZZA SANTO SPIRITO

(near the Pitti Palace, see plan of the monument N. 15)

On the corner of Via Mazzetta, observe the beautiful *Guadagni palace* with its splendid *loggia* (1503), attributed to Baccio d'Agnolo or Simone del Pallaiolo called "il Cronaca". This is an example of a typical Renaissance home. The small monument to the agronomist *Cosimo Ridolfi* in the Square is by Raffaello Romanelli (XIX cent.).

**Church of S. Spirito** (fig. 139). This was Brunelleschi's last creation begun in 1444, with its typical simple, geometric façade. The *belltower* is by Baccio d'Agnolo (1503-17); the *dome* by Salvi di Andrea (1479-81) following a design by Brunelleschi.

**Interior.** The church is in the form of a Latin cross with a nave and two aisles that continue in the transept with admirable proportions. Although Brunelleschi's original design underwent some alterations, the church reflects his architectural concept based on the harmony of proportions and on the measured division of space.
Along the walls of the church are 38 semi-circular chapels containing the works of art that are listed in the enclosed plan. The beautiful stained glass window of the inside façade is of the XV century.

**Fig. 139 - Church of Santo Spirito**

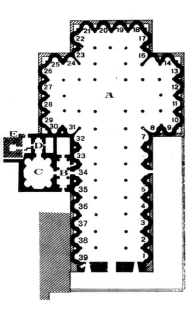

**PLAN OF S.SPIRITO**

A. High Altar by Caccini (1608)

B. Vestibule of the Sacristy

C. Sacristy

D. Offices of the Church

E. Bell-tower by Baccio d'Agnolo

**LATERAL CHAPELS**

1. Assumption and Saints by Pier Francesco di Jacopo (XVI cent.).

2. "Pietà" copy of 1549 of Michelangelo's in St. Peter's (Rome).

3. St. Nicholas of Tolentino, polychrome wood statue attributed to Nanni Unghero.

4. Christ driving the merchants from the temple by Stradano (1572).

5. Incoronation of the Virgin (XVII cent.).

6. Martyrdom of St. Stephen by Passignano.

7. Archangel Raphael and Tobit: marble group by Baratta (XVII cent.).

8. Crucifix with the Virgin and St. John (XVII cent.).

9. Transfiguration by Pier Francesco di Jacopo (XVI cent.).

10. Madonna del Soccorso in the manner of Cosimo Rosselli.

11. Buontalenti Chapel (1601) with small XIV cent. Crucifix.

12. Madonna and Child with Saints and the donors Tanai dei Nerli and his wife with a view of the Porta S. Frediano, by Filippino Lippi (XV cent.).

13. Apparition of the Virgin to St. Bernard, by Ficherelli.

14. Marriage of the Madonna (1713. Behind the grating, marble sarcophagus of Neri di Gino Capponi (political figure) (1388-1457), by Bernardo Rossellino (1458).

15. Madonna enthroned and Saints in the manner of Lorenzo di Credi.

16. Madonna and Child with Saints, XV cent., polyptych.

17. Epiphany by Leoni (XVI cent.).

18. On the altar, Holy Martyrs by Alessandro Allori (1575); in the predella a view of the Pitti Palace before it was enlarged.

19. The Adultress by A. Allori

20. The Blessed Chiara da Montefalco, XVI cent.

21. Annunciation, of the XV cent.

22. Nativity (school of Domenico Ghirlandaio).

23. Madonna and Child with Angel and Saints, XV cent. tablet with an original frame.

24. St. Monica creating the order of the Augustinian nuns (XV cent.) with an original frame.

25. Madonna and Child with Saints by Cosimo Rosselli (1481).

26. Chapel by A. Sansovino.

27. The Trinity worshipped by St. Catherine and Mary Magdalen, XV cent. attributed to Granacci.

28. Madonna enthroned with Saints, XV cent.

29. Madonna and Child with Saints by Carli (1504).

30. Christ bearing the Cross by Michele del Ghirlandaio. Above, a XV cent. stained glass window representing Incredulity of St. Thomas.

31. Madonna Enthroned with Saints, school of Fra Bartolomeo.

32. Madonna and Saints. Copy of an original by Rosso Fiorentino. XV cent. stained glass window.

33. Entrance to the beautiful vestibule of the Sacristy.

34. Madonna with St. Ann and other Saints by Ridolfo Ghirlandaio.

35. St. Thomas of Villanova distributing alms. XVII cent.

36. Blessed Giovanni da S. Fecondo by Masini (1691).

37. Statue of Christ, copy by Landini (1579) of the original by Michelangelo in the Church of Minerva in Rome.

38. Resurrection (XVI cent.).

In the lateral chapels, entering: *Deposition* and *Christ Resurrected*, copies of originals by Michelangelo in Rome. The Baroque *Tabernacle on the Chancel,* by Caccini (1599-1608), is not in keeping with the harmony of the church, Among the paintings observe, in the right transept, the *Virgin,* commissioned by Tanai de' Nerli, a powerful Florentine and adversary of Savonarola, work of Filippino Lippi; in the apse, *Madonna and Saints* by Lorenzo di Credi; in the last chapel of the choir, on the left: *Nativity,* from the school of Ghirlandaio.

In the left transept, in the first chapel (XXIV): *St. Monica who founds the Order of the Augustinians* by Botticini; in the following chapel, *Madonna and Saints* by Cosimo Rosselli. On the following altars are works by XVI century Florentine artists. For architecture and sculpture, observe chapel XXVII, early masterpiece by Andrea Sansovino (1492) who executed, in marble, *the Last Supper,* the Tabernacle and the *Stories of the Virgin.* The balustrade around the Chapel is from 1642. Farther ahead, under the organ, is the entrance to the famous *vestibule.*

**Vestibule**. Projected by Cronaca (Simone del Pollaiolo), it has beautiful Corinthian columns that sustain the splendid vault with stone locunars representing the *symbols of the Holy Spirit.* From here we pass to the

**Sacristy**. Its octagonal shape was inspired by the Baptistry and was built following a design by Giuliano da San Gallo (1489-92). The *Dome* was constructed from designs by Antonio del Pollaiolo and Salvi d'Andrea. Here you can admire the splendid wooden *Crucifix* by Michelangelo reallocated in the Sacristy after a recent restoration. Returning to the Square, on the left of the Church is the entrance to the *Refectory* with a fresco representing the *Last Supper* by Orcagna. This room is also enriched with valuable works of art donated by the antique dealer Salvatore Romano (1946).

In the morning, the piazza with its little market makes the folk customs of this area quite interesting. Going right on Via S. Agostino and taking the short Via S. Monaca, which intersects Via de' Serragli, we come to Piazza del Carmine, where from a distance we can admire the slender cupola of the church of S. Frediano attached to the Cestello seminary, by Antonio M. Ferri based on a design by Cerrutti (1698).

## CHURCH OF S. MARIA DEL CARMINE
(see plan of the monuments N. 16)

This was an old Romanesque church from 1268, but was remodelled in later centuries, after having been almost totally destroyed by the fire of 1771. Fortunately two chapels were saved; the Corsini Chapel on the left and, except for the ceiling, the famous Brancacci Chapel in the right transept.

**Interior.** In the form of a Latin cross with a single nave, it was reconstructed by Giuseppe Ruggeri and Giulio Mannaioni. The ample vault was frescoed, with a search for illusionistic effects in the architecture, by Domenico Stagi. The stained glass window of the inside façade is modern. At front of the Church, on the right is the *Brancacci Chapel.*

**The Brancacci Chapel:** constitutes one of the most solemn monuments to Italian Renaissance painting, because of the cycle of frescoes begun by Masolino da Panicale, continued by Masaccio and finished by Filippino Lippi (see plan). By Masolino da Panicale, Masaccio's teacher, delicate painter of late Gothic style who, in these frescoes, was certainly influenced by his young pupil Masaccio, we can admire: *The Temptation of Adam and Eve,* a great part of *St. Peter healing the cripple* and the *Resuscitation of Tabitha.*
Masaccio continued alone after Masolino left for Hungary and, in opposition to the *Temptation,* represents the *Expulsion of Adam and Eve*

**Figs. 140-141 - Masaccio: Head of St. Peter and Head of Christ (detail of the Tribute)**

161

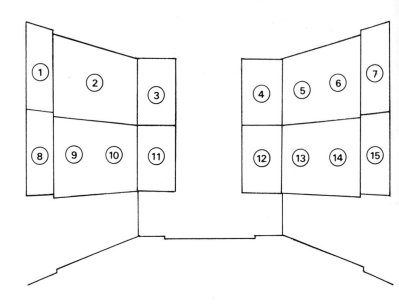

## BRANCACCI CHAPEL

1. Expulsion of Adam and Eve from Paradise (Masaccio).
2. Payment of the tribute (Masaccio) (plate LXIX).
3. St. Peter preaching (Masolino).
4. St. Peter baptizing (Masaccio).
5. St. Peter healing the cripple (Masaccio).
6. St. Peter resuscitates Tabitha (Masolino and Masaccio).
7. Temptation of Adam and Eve (Masolino).
8. St. Paul visits St. Peter in prison (Filippino Lippi).
9. St. Peter resuscitates the Emperor's son (Filippino Lippi).
10. St. Peter enthroned (Masaccio).
11. St. Peter healing with his shadow (Masaccio).
12. St. Peter and St. John giving alms (Masaccio).
13. Crucifixion of St. Peter (Filippino Lippi).
14. St. Peter and St. Paul before the Proconsul (Filippino Lippi).
15. Angel liberating St. Peter from prison (Filippino Lippi).

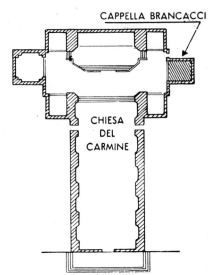

Figs. 142 - Brancacci Chapel - Masaccio: Adam and Eve

(fig. 142) with a new language. Among the most dramatic scenes of the Life of St. Peter is the celebrated *Payment of the Tribute* in which the young Masaccio surpasses his teacher in the powerful, monumental, and vibrantly chiaroscuro figures, full of profound humanity. We can admire the majestic scene in the ample landscape cleared by the light of a recent storm: "Christ the Man" dominates the "Apostles" (placed in a semicircle), shown in various attitudes. The story evolves in three times which correspond with three successive scenes. The most important is the one in the center, where the Master (fig. 141) orders St. Peter to pay the tribute by taking the money from the mouth of a fish. On the left, the landscape seems to disappear while, on the right the *Scene of the Tribute* is interrupted by the architecture of the buildings. In the scene of *St. Peter Enthroned,* by Masaccio, the young man below that looks out is believed to be a self-portrait of the artist. The cycle of frescoes, interrupted by Masaccio who went to Rome where he died (1429), was later continued in 1484 by the young Filippino Lippi, who finished the episode of *St. Peter who Resuscitates the Emperor's Grandson* (on the lower left wall; see plan N. 9). By the same artist are: *St. Peter visits St. Paul in prison* (no. 8). On the right wall: *Liberation of St. Peter from prison* (15); the young man on the left of the Angel is a self portrait of Filippino Lippi, who also executed *St. Peter and St. Paul before the Proconsul* and the *Crucifixion of St. Peter,* in which in the group of the *three young men,* he painted *a rare portrait of Botticelli (in profile),* his teacher, while the hillside of Bellosguardo is represented in the background. The scenes finished by the young Filippino, although quite different from Masaccio's drama and Masolino's archaism, are nonetheless enlivened by the artist's sensitivity, expecially acute in the physiognomical and psychological details of the personages. On the altar is an interesting *Madonna and Child* of the XIV cent.

Leaving the Chapel, the vestibule on the right leads to the vast XV cent. Sacristy containing works by Andrea da Firenze. The frescoes on the walls are by Bicci di Lorenzo representing *scenes* from the life of St. Cecilia.

Returning to the church, in the choir is the monument of Soderini, Gonfalonier of the Republic (he is buried in Rome), work of Benedetto da Maiano. In the left aisle is the Chapel of S. Andrea, bishop of Fiesole (1302-73), built by Silvani (1683). The Church has a beautiful XVII century cloister, which can be reached from the Sacristy via the room dedicated to illustrations of the "fresco" painting technique.

# FOURTH ITINERARY

*Piazza S. Firenze - Bargello Palace, National Museum - Church of Badia Fiorentina - Dante's House - Square and Church of S. Croce, Pazzi Chapel - Casa Buonarroti.* (This itinerary is indicated by numebrs 17, 18, 21 and 22 on the map of the monuments.)

## SQUARE AND CHURCH OF SAN FIRENZE

On the right, the large Baroque building, originally a convent of the Order of Filippo Neri, was built by Pier Francesco Silvani and Pietro da Cortona (XVII-XVIII cents.). Great part of the building is now the seat of the Tribunal. In the interior is the beautiful Courtyard by Borromini.

On the corner of Via Gondi is the Gondi Palace, with the magnificent courtyard by Giuliano da Sangallo (1490-94), a splendid example of a wealthy residence. Leonardo da Vinci lived here as a guest of the family.

## PALACE OF THE BARGELLO (fig. 143)

A Fortress-Palace, it was begun in 1255 as the seat of the Captain of the People. The architect of this building, still unknown, incorporated into the palace the existent embattled tower of the "Volognana" with its historic bell that announced the capital punishments with its dismal toll, and that now rings on the occasions of national or local holidays.

From 1261 the palace was the seat of the Podestà, the magistrate whose role was to maintain equilibrium between the parties, and later of the Guidici di Rota. From 1574 it was the seat of the Bargello or Captain of Justice. In this period the interior of the Palace was transformed into squallid and harsh prisons, located on the ground floor, in the "Loggia" and the "Salone" (Great Hall), then divided among 4 floors with more 30 cells. At the time of the Podestà, the Hall was the seat of the General Council. It is now dedicated to Donatello and contains masterpieces of XV century Florentine sculpture.

In the courtyard the scaffold was located (now replaced by the well). The room on the ground floor was once used for torture. The prisoners were forced to confess by the use of cruel and horrible instruments of torture. Grand Duke Peter of Lorraine abolished these infamous abuses of Justice, the sad prison cells, the scaffold, the instruments of torture that historians remember with horrifying description. With knowledgeable restorations by Francesco Mazzei (1865-71) the Palace, a splendid example of Florentine Gothic architecture, was brought back to its antique splendor.

Fig. 143

# NATIONAL MUSEUM

The Museum was started by the Provisional Government of Tuscany who in 1859 began the collection of statues and other works of art originally in the Uffizi, or coming from religious and public buildings which passed over to the State. The art collections were continuously enriched with the generous contributions of Carrand (1888), Ressman (1899), Franchetti (1909) and others which were added to the new acquisitions made by the State. Because of the valuable art collections, this Museum is considered among the most important, especially for Renaissance sculpture.

The old torture chamber at the foot of the stairs, an austere place with wide vaults supported on robust pillars. On the walls, *Madonna and Saints,* a fresco of the XIV Century (restored). The room is dedicated to Florentine sculpture of the XVI Century, and to Michelangelo in particular. Passing through the room from left to right: Admirable works by Michelangelo include: the *Drunken Bacchus with the Small Satyr nibbling a Grape* (about 1498), the first completely round work known by this master, clearly in imitation of older art; the small *David* (about 1531 and not to be confused with the one in the Academy); the

**Fig. 144 - Courtyard of the Bargello (National Museum)**

167

dramatic *Bust of Brutus* (1540), inspired by Roman models; the *"Pitti Tondo"* representing the Madonna and Child and St. Giovannino, contemporary with the David (1504). There follow, the *"Drunken Bacchus"* by Sansovino and a series of terracotta models of works by Michelangelo, executed by his pupils. Worthy of note is the *Leda and the Swan* by Ammannati which is a reproduction of a lost picture by Michelangelo. On the Via del Proconsolo side of the room: *Adam and Eve* by Bandinelli; the *Dying Adonis* by Vincenzo Danti; *Virtue overcomes Vice*, by Giambologna; the *Victory of Florence over Pisa*, statues on clearly manneristic lines. An outstanding example of elegance and refinement is the celebrated *Mercury* (Fig. 145) in which one notes the energetic curvature of the body, and various works by Cellini: the statuettes which at one time were in the niches around the base of the Perseus (of which a model of the first version is on show), the relief of *Perseus freeing Andromeda*; the grandiose *Bronze Bust of Cosimo I.* (Fig. 151) previously on the Fortress of Portaferraio. The marble statue which has deteriorated with time, from the Boboli Gardens, is a *Narcisus,* a great rarity in Cellini's works, which generally used wax for bronze castings.

Beside the door to the vestibule: Bronze Bust of Michelangelo, by his pupil and friend Daniele da Volterra, which has often been reproduced.

**Courtyard** (fig. 144). Walking around the courtyard one can better admire the pictorial effect caused by the deep shadows of the harmonious Loggia. The area is rendered solemn by the splendid *staircase,* by Neri di Fioravanti (1345), enriched at the top by the beautiful *portal* and *gate* by Giuliano da Sangallo (XV cent.). On the wall are crests of the various Podestà and Giudici di Rota who lived here. Under the portico, crest of the Quarters and various sections of the city. Of interest is the *lantern* in the form of a cornucopia, in wrought iron by Guido Serafini (XVI cent.). On the other side of the courtyard is the large statue of *Ocean* by Giambologna; *The Canon of St. Paul* with the Apostle's head, by Cenni (1638). In the center of the courtyard is the octagonal well that replaced the scaffold. Opposite to the entrance under the portico we enter the room containing XIV century sculpture. Returning to the courtyard, on the left is a more comfortable staircase that leads to the **first floor**, in the **Hall of the Ivories**. Among the most important works we point out, near the window, a rare French *chess board* from the Carrand Collection and, against the entrance wall, *Madonna and Child* (Umbrian art of the XIV-XV cent.).

On the left enter the:

Fig. 145 - Giambologna: Mercury
Fig. 146 - Donatello: Young David in bronze
Fig. 147 - Cellini: Ganymede
Fig. 148 - Donatello: St. George

**Room on the left of the Balcony.** It contains precious liturgical objects of XIV-XV cent. Tuscan art, a *reliquary bust* of St. Ignatius and a *silver cross* (Tuscan art of the XVI cent.).

On the left is the ample:

**Hall of the Majolicas.** In the first case: rare *Spanish-Moorish majolicas* with metallic reflections; in the other cases are ceramics made in Florence, Urbino, Pesaro etc, in prevalence of the XVI cent. At the end of the room: *Credence* in walnut with intarsia design, Florentine art. XVI cent.; above is a *Garland* with the insignias of the Bartolini and Medici families, in *glazed terra cotta* by Giovanni della Robbia. Returning to the previous room, we then pass (as shown in table LXX) to the splendid:

**Loggia or Balcony** that contains works by the Flemish artist Giambologna (1524-1608). Among these we can admire the realistic *animals* which come from the Medici Gardens, and the statue of *Architecture.*

**Great Hall** with the cross vaults supported by robust octagonal pilasters that, in height, occupies the two floors, which was once the seat of the Grand Council at the time of the Podestà. The Hall is now dedicated to the sculptures of Donatello, among which stands out, in the niche of the far wall, *St. George* (c. 1410 - fig. 148), originally in the church of Orsanmichele, perhaps the first Renaissance work of the Master. Also on display by this great artist is the David in bronze (c. 1430 - fig. 146), soft and palpitating, showing his attentive observation of reality. It can be considered an idealized portrait of a Florentine urchin. By Donatello is the youthful *St. John the Baptist* in marble, made for the Martelli family (c. 1440). On the right of the St. George, a realistic bust with a medallion, inspired by classical art, that because of its bold plasticity, is called the "son of Gattamelata". On the left is a *Crucifixion* from the artist's last period; next is a *bust of St. John,* by Desiderio da Settignano. On the right wall, famous bronze reliefs representing the *Sacrifice of Isaac,* by Brunelleschi and Ghiberti, made for the contest for the second doors of the Baptistry. The confrontation of these two panels is particularly interesting. Between these two panels is a bas-relief representing a *Battle of Roman and Barbarian soldiers* by Bertoldo, teacher of Michelangelo. Below, a bronze reliquary chest by Ghiberti. Against the opposite wall are two bas-reliefs in marble and one in colored terra cotta by Agostino di Duccio. Around the sides of the room are delicate works by Desiderio da Settignano and other artists. By Donatello we also mention the *David* and young *St. John* in marble, the *Lion* (Marzocco) in stone believed to be a copy of a lost original. Finally, by

**Fig. 149 - Luca Della Robbia: Madonna**
**Fig. 150 - Giotto: Portrait of Dante Alighieri**

Donatello, is the smiling bronze *Putto.* On the entrance wall is a Madonna and Child by Michelozzo. By Luca Della Robbia (1400-82) we admire the *Madonna della Mela* (fig. 149), the *Madonna del Roseto* and two marble bas-reliefs, with episodes from the *Life of St. Peter.* By the Sienese painter and sculptor Vecchietta (1412-80) is the bronze sepulchral statue of Mariano Sozzino, a Sienese judge. From the far end of the room we pass to the:

**Tower Room.** In show cases, various objects of Arabian manufacture or at least of oriental provenance. The fifteenth century *mosque lamp,* in enamelled glass is a great rarity.

**Hall of the Podestà.** In this room the Podestà rendered justice. Also called room of the Duke of Athens because, during the restorations, his crest with the "two-tailed Lion" came to light, having been covered after his expulsion (1343). In the center of the room is a bronze bust of the collector Carrand (1888) who willed to the Museum furniture, *German, Flemish and Italian paintings,* rare and precious objects from the XV and XVI century. Also displayed are exquisite statuettes and wrought gold objects from Italian, French and Flemish art of the XIV-XVII centuries. In the glass cases at the end are XVI cent. Limoges enamels, and XV-XVII cent. glass crystal. Next is the:

**Figs. 151-152 - Cellini: Bust of Cosimo I - Andrea della Robbia: Little Boy**

**Chapel of the Podestà.** The Chapel has a barrel vaulted ceiling, illuminated by acute arched windows, and is where the condemned passed their last night in prayer. The frescoes represent: on the opposite wall, *Vision of Paradise;* on the lateral walls, Scenes from the life of the *Madonna and St. John the Baptist*; on the entrance wall, *Vision of the Inferno.* These frescoes which were whitewashed during the plague of 1630 and brought to light by the English scholar Seymour Kirkup in 1839-40, were badly restored by Martini and have lost all their iconographical value. Even in the Vision of Paradise, attributed to Giotto, the *portrait of Dante* (fig. 150) has been altered. Below, in the corner, is a *bust of the Poet* (Dante), drawn by Kirkup. Below the Paradise fresco on the left, *St. Jerome,* fresco by Bartolomeo di Giovanni. On the right, *Madonna and Child,* by Mainardi (1490), and in the center, tablet representing the *Madonna and Child between St. Francis and St. John Baptist,* by Giovanni Francesco (XV cent.), from the Carrand collection.

The magnificent lateral choir-stalls and central lectern, originally in San Miniato, are by Bernardo della Cecca (1438-98). In the cases against the entrance wall, Missals in two volumes, by Gherardo and Monte di Giovanni (XV cent.); above, four inlaid wood candelabras, end of XV century; right, *Pietà,* attributed to Jacopo della Quercia. Returning to the Hall of the Ivories, farther ahead on the left is the staircase leading to the:

**Fig 153 - Bargello (third floor) - Verrocchio: Bronze David**

**Second floor Room of Cellini and Giovanni della Robbia.**
By Cellini, goldsmith and sculptor, who also wrote a famous "Autobiography" we admire, on the left: small portrait of Grand Duke Francesco I, donated to his second wife Bianca Capello, with the card that accompagnied the gift. Next is an oval plaque with a bas-relief of a *greyhound.*

On the right wall, two refined *Ganymedes,* one is a restored classical statue, and the other, in bronze by Cellini, has the typical manneristic elegance. The room also contains works by Giovanni della Robbia (1469-1529), son of Andrea and nephew of Luca. With his popular type work, Giovanni puts an end to the highest level reached by glazed terracotta.

Continuing to the right and walking toward the entrance, we pass into the

**Room of Andrea della Robbia** (1435-1525), (nephew of Luca and father of Giovanni), whose splendid terra-cottas are displayed here, among them a bust of a boy (fig. 152).

**Room of Verrocchio** (1435-1588). Sculptor of delicate pictorial effects that constitute the origins of his pupil Leonardo da Vinci's great painting. By Verrocchio is the bronze *adolescent David* (fig. 153). Against the left wall *bust of a Gentlewoman with a nosegay,* believed to be Lucrezia Donati, loved by Lorenzo the Magnificent. Following are the *death of Francesca Tornabuoni, Madonna and Child* and the dramatic *Resurrection* in terra cotta. By Antonio del Pollaiolo (1429-98) is the small *Hercules and Antaeus,* with its nervous line suggesting volume and movement. Among the other works in the room are those by Benedetto da Maiano; by Francesco Laurana, *Bust of the Duke of Urbino* rendered with refined geometric abstraction. Against the far wall: among various *portrait-busts of noble Florentines* is the famous roundel with the *Madonna and Child* by Antonio Rossellino. Against the entrance wall, by Mino da Fiesole: marble busts of *Piero and Giovanni dei Medici;* above, Madonna and Child, fine low-relief with traces of gilding. Against the small right wall: *Faith, Ecce Homo* and *Portrait of an Unknown gentleman* by the refined Lucchese sculptor Matteo Civitali (1435-1501).

Ahead is the entrance to the **Hall of Chinery-piece.** This room is dedicated to artists particularly well known for small bronzes.

Noteworthy are those by Riccio, Bellano, Antico, Bandinelli, Giambologna, Francavilla, Soldani, Pietro di Barga and others. In front of the window, the *Dwarf Morgante*, by Giambologna originally on the loggia facing Piazza della Signoria. The glass cases contain fine collections of small bronzes, of classical inspiration, some grotesques, and small Italian plaques of the XV and XVI Centuries. At the end of the room,

*Anatomic Figure*, a bronze by Ludovico Cigoli (1559-1613).

The splendid Fifteenth Century gray stone chimney piece in Casa Borgherini, with the story of Cyrus and Croesus, by Benedetto da Rovezzano.

On the same floor but on the other side, one finds the:

**Arms Hall.** This contains a rich collection of Medieval and Renaissance arms, once the property of the Medici Grand Dukes from Cosimo the First to Cosimo the Third, or acquired by the Medici from della Rovere legacies. Of particular note are the diamond point *armour* of Francesco Maria della Rovere, and that of Cosimo III de' Medici, chiselled and burnished. In the show case opposite the entrance, the famous *Lamina di Agilulfo*, represents the triumph of the Lombard king (590 - 616), inspired by imperial models. Leaving the Museum, on Via Proconsolo, across the street is:

## CHURCH OF THE BADIA FIORENTINA

This was originally a Benedictine church founded in the XI century by Willa, mother of Ugo, Marquis of Tuscany. Enlarged at the end of the XIII century it acquired numerous additions in the XIV cent. In 1625 it was entirely remodelled by Matteo Segaloni. The entrance is through the beautiful portal by Benedetto da Rovezzano (1475), surmounted by

**Fig. 154 - House of Dante Alighieri**

**Fig. 155 - Church of Santa Croce - Giotto: Death of St. Francis**

*Madonna and Child* in glazed terra cotta by Buglioni (early XVI cent.).
The Vestibule, consisting of the beautiful portico with Corinthian columns, is by Benedetto da Rovezzano (1495).

**Interior of the Church.** It is the only church in Florence made in the form of a Greek cross. The beautiful carved ceiling is by Gamberai, following the design by Segaloni (1625). On the left wall, *Madonna appearing to St. Bernard,* masterpiece by Filippino Lippi (1485, on board). In the left wing *Tomb of Count Ugo, Marquis of Tuscany,* an extremely refined work by Mino da Fiesole (1480). Above, *Ascension* by Vasari. On the right wall, *Madonna and Child with St. Lawrence and St. Leonard,* delicate altar-back by Mino da Fiesole. In the right wing: *Tomb of Giannozzo Pandolfini,* from the school of Rossellino. Dante, who lived nearby, attended this church.

Passing through the choir on the right, we ascend to the upper portico of the *Cloister degli Aranci* (of the Oranges), which is frescoed with *Stories of St. Benedict* by Giovanni Consalvo (XV cent.). A visit to this picturesque cloister is particularly recommended because of the characteristic medieval atmosphere that is conserved here. From here we can best admire the hexagonal *bell-tower,* attributed to Arnolfo di Cambio, with its XIV cent. romanesque mullioned windows that terminate with a sharp cusp sustained by the beautiful cornice. Returning to Rovezzano's portico, we then go out to Via Dante Alighieri. On the lefts we reach the nearby little square of St. Margherita where we see the so-called *House of Dante:*

## HOUSE OF DANTE

The house is an arbitrary reconstruction of the last century (fig. 154), and is now used for displaying and selling contemporary art. On the Via St. Margherita side, in a medieval environment, we can visit the new Dante Museum consisting of documents and curios concerning Dante in Florence and in exile. According to recent documentation, it seems that Dante was born in a house on this little Square of San Martino on the same side as the restaurant "Il Pennello", so-called because it was opened as a wine cellar by the painter Albertinelli, and was a gathering place for artists of the time. Above the restaurant is the *terracotta medallion* with the portrait of the painter who abandoned art to dedicate himself to this business. In the square of S. Martino we see the "Torre della Castagna" (Tower of the Cestnut), that was the seat of local government, now occupiedi by offices of patriotic associations. Opposite is the Church of SAN MARTINO where Dante married Gemma Donati. The tiny church was reconstructed in the XV century. On the inside walls are frescoes with *stories of S. Martino and works of Charity,* by Domenico Ghirlandaio and Filippino Lippi. Here St. Antonino, beloved bishop of the Florentines, founded the famous "Compagnia dei Buonomini" who effectively helped the poor families and those of fallen fortune in the most unobtrusive manner, without humiliating the beneficiaries as stated in the Gospel: "that the right hand should not know what the left hand does".

Passing the front of the small but extremely interesting Dante Museum, one enters Via Santa Margherita, with the small church where, according to tradition, Dante met Beatrice; and eventually arrives in Via del Corso, the ancient Decumanus maximus. The **Church of Santa Maria de' Ricci** with an elegant Renaissance portico, founded in the fourteenth century, is half way along the street. The interior of the church, a charming example of the Baroque style, is well worth a visit; it contains a detached fresco of the Annunciation, of the Giotto school, on the High Altar.

Walking along the Via dei Magazzini, with its medieval buildings, we arrive at the nearby Via Condotta, with its old "tower-houses". Turning to the left we reach Piazza S. Firenze. Crossing the street, alongside the church, is the Via dell'Anguillara that crosses, ahead on the right, the picturesque Via Filippina. Still farther ahead is Via Bentaccordi, where on the façade of the modest house on the right corner, a plaque commemorates the place where Michelangelo lived as a boy. The beautiful palace that follows the curve of the Little Via Torta, actually stands on the outer line of the Roman Theatre which once stood on this site (behind the Palazzo Vecchio). Farther ahead is,

## PIAZZA SANTA CROCE

On the left corner at the beginning of Via Verdi, observe the beautiful Serristori, formerly Cocchi Palace, by Baccio d'Agnolo (c. 1520, now a school). Across the street, at the beginning of the square, is a gracious fountain (XVI cent.), used as a watering place for horses.

On the right is the large Palazzo dell'Antella, formerly Cerchi Palace (1619), with its façade frescoed by Giovanni da Sangiovanni and helpers (according to legend, in only 20 days).

Observe this palace and the one beside it which, supported on corbels, jut over the square. Under the corbels of the first palace is a bust of Cosimo II; below is a marble disk dated February 10, 1565 that marks the central point of the field when the soccer game was played in the square. In medieval times great crowds gathered in this famous square to hear the sermons of followers of St. Francis, among whom was St. Bernardine of Siena. Among the famous jousting tournaments held here, we mention that in honor of the "handsome Giuliano" Medici, presided over as queen by the "beautiful Simonetta", who was immortalized by Botticelli in his "Springtine" and "Birth of Venus" in the Uffizi.

**Fig. 156 - Church of Santa Croce (Holy Cross)**

## CHURCH OF SANTA CROCE

The church was begun, it is believed, by Arnolfo in 1294, on the site of an older church. The mediocre Façade by Niccolò Matas (1845-63 - fig. 156) contrasts with the simple and austere construction. The statues that decorate it are: by Giovanni Duprè, the *Madonna* above the central portal and the *Triumph of the Cross* in the lunette below; by Zocchi is the *Vision of Costantine* in the lunette of the right hand door; by Tito Sarrocchi is the *Discovery of the Cross* in the lunette of the left door.

The sandstone Gothic-style bell tower is Baccani (1874). On the left side is the beautiful XIV century portico in the same style as the one on the right, visible when entering the cloister. To the left of the façade is the mediocre monument dedicated to Dante Alighieri, by Enrico Pazzi (1865), which originally encumbered the center of the square but was

**Fig. 157 - Church of Santa Croce - Interior**
**Fig. 158 - Donatello - Wooden Crucifix (detail)**

removed in May 1968, and placed here after much controversial discussion.

**Interior** (fig. 157). In the form of a "T", its length is 115,43 meters, width 38,23 meters, width of the transept 73 meters. It is a vast and very simple church capable of holding much of the population of this crowded quarter. A solid construction, its octagonal stone pillars prolonged by strips sustains the beautiful trestled ceiling. The simple chapels in the transept accentuate the vertical value of the wide central nave and the pictorial effect is extended to the side aisles by means of the succession of transversal arches that sustain the beautiful vault with the sloping roof.

Originally all the walls were frescoed by the most famous XIV century artists. Cosimo I, after becoming absolute ruler of the city and insensitive to the glories of the past, had the famous frescoes covered with whitewash, and had Vasari add the heavy altars (with XVII cent. paintings) that contrast with the harmony of the church. Because of these altehations the frescoes were lost except for a few fragments that are conserved in the Museum in the Cloister. Before the church was declared "Pantheon of the nation's glories", many noble families were buried here thus reaching the number of 280 tombs. Now only famous Italians

Fig. 159

# PLAIN OF THE CHURCH OF SANTA CROCE

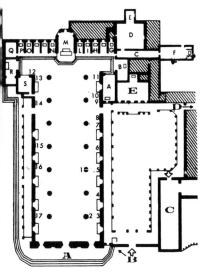

**Interior of the Church**

A. Castellani Chapel.
B. Baroncelli Chapel.
C. Entrance to the Sacristy.
D. Sacristy.
E. Rinuccini Chapel.
F. Novitiate Chapel.
G. Velluti Chapel.
H. Giugni Chapel.
I. Peruzzi Chapel.
L. Bardi Chapel.
M. High Altar.
N. Tosinghi Chapel.
O. Pulci Chapel.
P. Bardi di Vernio Chapel.
Q. Niccolini Chapel.
R. Bardi Chapel.
S. Salviati Chapel.

1. Pulpit by B. da Maiano (central nave).
2. Madonna del Latte.
3. Tomb of Michelangelo.
4. Monument to Dante.
5. Tomb of Vittorio Alfieri.
6. Tomb of Machiavelli.
7. Tomb of Lanzi.
8. Tabernacle of Donatello.
9. Tomb of Leonardo Bruni.
10. Tomb of Gioacchino Rossini.
11. Statue of Ugo Foscolo.
12. Monument to Cherubini.
13. Tomb of Morghen.
14. Tomb of Carlo Marsuppini.
15. Pietà (Bronzino).
16. Monumental slab of Lorenzo and Vittorio Ghiberti.
17. Tomb of Galileo Galilei.

A. Entrance to the Church.
B. Entrance to the Cloister.
C. Museum.
D. Entrance to the second Cloister.
E. Pazzi Chapel.

can be buried here; the last of these being inventor Barsanti buried in 1954.

**Central nave.** On the third pillar (see plan N. 1) is the famous *pulpit* (fig. 159) by Benedetto da Maiano (1472-76) with panels representing the *Stories of St. Francis* (inspired by those of Ghiberti) and the *Cardinal Virtues* below.

**Right Aisle.** Tomb of Michelangelo (fig. 169), by Vasari (1570). The figures of *Painting, Sculpture* and *Architecture* are by Lorenzi, Cioli and Giovanni dell'Opera (XVI cent.). The *bust of the Artist* was taken from his death mask. In front of the tomb, on the first pillar, *Madonna and Child* called "of the milk" (fig. 161), a delicate low-relief by Antonio Rossellino (1578). Between the second and third altars, a *Cenotaph to Dante Alighieri* (who died and is buried in Ravenna), by Stefano Ricci (1829); between the third and fourth altars, monument to Vittorio Alfieri by Canova (1810), in neoclassical style; between the fourth and fifth altars, *Tomb of Niccolò Machiavelli,* by Innocenzo Spinazzi (1787), with the profile of Machiavelli on the plaque being held by the allegori-

**Fig. 160 - Vasari: Tomb of Michelangelo**
**Fig. 161 - Antonio Rossellino - Madonna "of the milk"**

cal figure of *Diplomacy.*

After the tomb of the art historian Luigi Lanzi, is the celebrated *Tabernacle by Donatello* (fig. 162) in gilded grey-stone (pietra serena), with the magnificent *Annunciation,* and above, vivacious *putti* in terracotta. Following is the *tomb* of the humanist and chancellor of the Florentine Republic Leonardo Bruni, that became the prototype of Renaissance tombs because of its harmony and serene composition. Next is the tomb, by Cassioli, of Gioacchino Rossini who died in Paris and was transported here in 1866. Finally, by Berti (1936), is the *statue of Ugo Foscolo* who sang the praises of Santa Croce in his poem "Sepolcri", and who is buried under the floor, as indicated by the inscription.

**Right wing of the transept.** *Tomb of Prince Neri Corsini,* by Fantacchiotti.

**Castellani or Sacrament Chapel.** This chapel still conserves a great part of the XIV century fresco decoration. On the right wall: *Stories of St. Nicholas of Bari and St.John the Baptist;* on the left are *Storie of St.John the Evangelist and St. Anthony Abbot,* all by Agnolo Gaddi, son of Taddeo, and helpers. The *Crucifix* is by Niccolò di Pietro Gerini (1386). On the left entrance wall, surmounted by a very fine grating with figures of the *Archangel and the Virgin* is the *tomb* of a member of the Giugni family, attributed to the Sienese Balduccio (XIV cent.).

Fig. 162 - Church of Santa Croce - Donatello: Annunciation

185

**Baroncelli now Giugni Chapel.** The famous frescoes, which have been carefully restored, are by Taddeo Gaddi (1332-38), faithful pupil of Giotto, who represented *Stories from the Life of the Virgin* showing a fine ability for narration. On the right end wall, *Madonna of the Girdle,* by Sebastiano Mainardi (XV cent.). Leaving this chapel to the right we pass the beautiful portal and enter the corridor with the barrel vaulted ceiling and elegant mullioned windows, by Michelozzo who, in 1434, also built the Chapel at the end called "Novitiate" or "Medici" Chapel, because it was built for Cosimo the Elder. The harmonious chapel contains various Della Robbia works. On the right of the corridor is the entrance to the *Sacristy.* On the walls are *Stories of the Passion,* frescoes attributed to Niccolo di Pietro Gerini (end of the XIV cent.). Separated by the "wrought-iron gate" is the small,

**Rinuccini Chapel.** Frescoed by Giovanni da Milano and helpers (c. 1365), with *Stories of Mary Magdalen* on the right wall; *Stories of Mary* on the left wall; and in the vault, the *Saviour* and the *Evangelists.* Among the collaborators we mention the one known to the critics as the "Master of the Rinuccini Chapel", whose style is near to that of Nardo di Cione. On the altar is a *polyptych* with the *Madonna, Child and Saints* by Giovanni del Biondo (1397).

Returning to the church we mention the fact that the eleven chapels in the transept were altered or remodelled in the XIV century by the noble families for their burial places.

I. VELLUTI CHAPEL. Conserves fragments of XIII century frescoes with Legends of St. Michael the Archangel.

II. CALDERINI CHAPEL later Riccardi. The vault was frescoed by Giovanni da S. Giovanni.

III. GIUGNI CHAPEL later Bonaparte. On the left, *tomb of Carlotta Bonaparte* by Lorenzo Bartolini; on the right, *Tomb of Giulia Bonaparte Clary* (d. 1845), by Pampaloni.

IV. PERUZZI CHAPEL. Frescoed by Giotto probably around 1320. It underwent an unfortunate restoration by Marini (1863) and was once again restored in 1965: On the walls, fragments of the *Stories of St. John the Evangelist*; on the sides of the windows, *four Saints.*

V. BARDI CHAPEL. Entirely frescoed by Giotto after 1317 with *Stories of St. Francis.* Unfortunately even these frescoes, discovered in 1840, were unhappily restored by Gaetano Bianchi. With the restoration of 1965 the parts which were not original were removed, leaving those which the experts believe to be by Giotto (who can be appreciated in the fullnes of his form in the famous Madonna, located in the Uffizi Gallery). Among the remains of these frescoes that narrate the *Stories*

Fig. 163 - Museum of Santa Croce - Cimabude: Crucifix - Before the Flood of 1966 (big photo) and after (small photo)

*of St. Francis,* we point out the *Death of the Saint* (fig. 155 pag. 176-177, 1318). The altar-piece with Stories of St. Francis is believed to be by a Florentine artist influenced by Byzantine art (c. 1265).

VI. MAIN CHAPEL. This chapel is rendered light by the verticalism of its form illuminated by tall beautiful stained-glass windows, and was frescoed by Agnolo Gaddi. On the altar, polyptych composed of panels from dismembered works by various Florentine artists of the late XIV century. In the center is the *Madonna* by Niccolò di Pietro Gerini; flanked by *Doctors of the Church* by Nardo di Cione; unknown is the artist of the predella. Above is a large Crucifix by a follower of Giotto. The walls, entirely frescoed by Agnolo Gaddi and followers (1380-85) representing the famous *Legend of the Cross* (fig. 164) narrated with richness of personages, minutely detailed and with the poetic language of Florentine-Gothic painting.

On the right wall the scenes show, from top to bottom: Seth receives a branch from the tree of life from St. Michael; Seth plants the branch on the tomb of Adam; The Queen of Sheba adoring the bridge made from the wood of the tree; Solomon has the tree buried; the Jews extract the tree from the pool in which it is found and make it into a cross; Saint Helena finds the three crosses, among which is the "true Cross" which will be identified by means of a miracle.

On the left wall, from top to bottom: St. Helena carries the cross in procession into Jerusalem; Chosroes, King of the Persians, conquers Jerusalem, carries away the Cross and is adored by his subjects; an Angel announces to Heraclius his coming victory; Heraclius defeats Chosroes and has him beheaded; an Angel appears to Heraclius warning him that he must abandon triumphs and honors; Heraclius gets down from his horse and, carrying the Cross in penitant's robes, enters Jerusalem. In the vault are figures of the *Saviour,* the *Evangelists* and *Saint Francis.*

VII. TOSINGHI CHAPEL later SPINELLI AND SLOANE. Remodelled at the beginning of the XIX cent. On the altar is a polyptych of the *Madonna and Saints* by Giovanni del Biondo (XIV cent.). The predella with historical scenes is by Neri di Bicci.

VIII. CHAPEL OF ST. ANN. Restored, it is dedicated to the "Italian Mother and to the Unknown Soldier". The monument is by Libero Andreotti (1926).

IX. CHAPEL OF ST. ANTHONY OF PADUA. Renovated in 1826.

X. PULCI CHAPEL later Berardi later BARDI. Frescoes of the *Martyrdom of St. Lawrence* and the *Martyrdom of St. Stephen* by Bernardo Daddi and helpers (c. 1330, restored). On the altar a large terracotta work by Giovanni della Robbia showing the *Madonna and Child* be-

**Fig. 165 - Monument to Galileo Galilei**
**Fig. 166 - Tomb of Gioacchino Rossini**

tween Mary Magdalen and St. John the Evangelist.

XI: BARDI DI VERNIO CHAPEL. On the walls are celebrated frescoes by Maso di Banco (c. 1340, restored) representing *Stories of St. Sylvester* and of *Constantine:* among these, the *Miracle of the bull resuscitated by the Saint, the Dreams of Constantine* with the Vision of SS. Peter and Paul. The *Final Judgement* is from the school of Maso, the *Deposition* in the manner of Taddeo Gaddi. On the altar, a panel by Jacopo di Cione with *St. Giovanni Gualberto and episodes from his life.*

XII. NICCOLINI CHAPEL, at the end of the transept, (closed by the gate), by Giovanni Dosio; the vault was frescoed by Volterrano (XVII cent.).

XIII. BARDI CHAPEL (closed by the gate). It contains Donatello's famous Wooden Crucifix (c. 1425 - fig. 158).

XIV. SALVIATI CHAPEL, rebuilt by Gherardo Silvani (XVII cent.). Contains the harmonious tomb of Princess Sophia Zamoyska, by Bartolini (1840). Descending the steps we see the *Monument to Luigi Cherubini,* musician who died and is buried in Paris, by Fantacchiotti (1869). In front of the first pillar is a *statue of Leon Battista Alberti* by Bartolini (1840). From this spot, observe the beautiful rose-window of the internal façade with the *Deposition.*

**Left Aisle.** Monument to the engraver Raffaello Morghen by Odoardo Fantacchiotti (1854). The painting in the next altar is the *Pentacost* by Vasari. The three medallions are in memory of *Christopher Columbus, Amerigo Vespucci* and the astronomer *Paolo Toscanelli.* Following is the famous tomb of *Carlo Marsuppini,* humanist and Secretary of the Florentine Republic, by Desiderio da Settignano (1469), who, inspired by the famous tomb of Leonardo Bruni by Rossellino, directly opposite, made the forms more delicate, as shown by the figures of the children which are considered among the most admirable creations of the Renaissance. In the floor, also by Desiderio, *monumental slab of Gregorio Marsuppini,* father of Carlo. On the wall, above left, fragment of a fresco by Agnolo Gaddi. Following: monument to the great hydraulics engineer and statesman Vittorio Fossombroni (d. 1844), by Bartolini (1850). Ahead is a medallion with a *bust of Donatello* (buried in San Lorenzo). Below: monument to *Carlo Botta.* On the fifth altar, *Ascension* by Stradano (1569). Followed by a *Pietà* by Bronzino. In the floor, large *monumental slab* (with inscription) of *Lorenzo Ghiberti,* who is buried here with his son Vittorio. The next small slab is of Barsanti, remembered also on the wall above. On the wall, follow the plaques of Raphael (buried in the Pantheon) and of *Leonardo* (buried in Amboise restored) and the tomb of *Galileo Galilei* (d. 1642) erected following the design of Giulio Foggini (fig. 165). The statues of *Astronomy* and *Geometry* are by Vincenzo Foggini and Gerolamo Ticciati; the *bust of Galileo* by Foggini.

**Internal façade.** The beautiful stained glass rose-window previously mentioned, is by the Florentine Giovanni del Ponte (1399-1437). Below, on the right of the central door, the *monument to the historian Gino Capponi* is by Bortone (1884); on the left of the door, by Pio Fedi (1883) in the *monument to G. Battista Niccolini,* buried between the second and third pillars of the right aisle. The statue of *Liberty that breaks the chains,* in remembrance of Niccolini who was a strong advocate of Liberty, inspired Bartholdi who sculptured the famous Statue of Liberty in New York harbor, offered to America by France. Leaving the church, on the left is the entrance to the Cloister of Santa Croce.

## CLOISTER OF SANTA CROCE

The vision offered by this first Cloister (fig. 167) is stupendous, especially on clear mornings. From every angle we can admire the harmonious XIV century construction, closed on the far end by the portico of the Pazzi Chapel. Beginning the visit, under the portico on the right,

**Fig. 164 - Old Refectory - T. Gaddi: The Tree of the Holy Cross and the Last Supper**

*Tomb of Girolamo Segato* who, dying at the age of 45 years (1835), condemned by the Inquisition, destroyed his invention of the petrification of animals and cadavers. In the niche is the small symbolic monument to Florence Nightingale (born in Florence, 1820-1890)), by Sargent. During the restoration, some badly damaged frescoes and numerous plaques that overpowered the XIV cent. style were removed. However the harmony of the Cloister would be further improved if the statue of the *Almighty* by Bandinelli were also taken away.

**Pazzi chapel** (the interior is described farther ahead) with its simple geometric façade left incomplete because of the death of Brunelleschi (1446), who began its construction in 1430. After his death it was continued by his collaborators who left the pronaos incomplete, resting on Corinthian columns, which sustain the high attic divided into squares, interrupted in the center by the perfect curve of the arch. Farther ahead, on the right of the cloister, is the entrance to the Museum of the Opera di Santa Croce.

## MUSEUM OF THE OPERA DI SANTA CROCE

Many works of this museum were damaged in the flood of November 1966. Among these we mention the famous Crucifix by Cimabue (fig.

163 - page 187). On the left wall a fresco by Domenico Veneziano, originally in the Church, with St. Francis and St. John the Baptist. In a reconstruction of its original niche in Orsanmichele: the gilded bronze statue of St. Ludovic of Toulouse, young work of Donatello (c. 1422), already permeated by Renaissance classicism in the monumental yet sweet figure of the Saint. Proceeding ahead, on the right and left walls, are fragments of frescoes taken from the Church. On the end wall of this old refectory is the fresco by Taddeo Gaddi (restored) representing the *Tree of the Holy Cross;* below is the *Last Supper and other Stories.*

In the adjoining small room on the left, seat of the "Theological Studies for Laymen" are fragments of XV century windows; on the end wall, *Dying St. Francis distributes bread to his fellow monks,* fresco by Giovanni da San Giovanni. On the left of this room is a collection of paintings of the XVI and XVII centuries. Returning to the Cloister, farther ahead on the right, through the beautiful portal by Michelozzo or Benedetto da Maiano (c. 1459), we enter the

**Second Cloister,** that modern critics believe to be by Bernardo Rossellino (1409-64). Moving around this Renaissance Cloister we can better admire the extremely elegant portico surmounted by the light Loggia. From here we can see the " Rotunda" with, on the left, the tower of the *National Library,* one of the most important in Italy, with its entrance on Piazza dei Cavalleggeri, along the river, by Cesare Bazzani (1911-35). The National Library, very badly damaged during the flood, contains the richest collections of manuscripts and literary material printed in Italy. Returning to the first Cloister, observe the tall cusps along the side of the Church, that enrich the XIV century portico closed by the Pazzi Chapel (fig. 167).

## PAZZI CHAPEL

Last creation by Brunelleschi, left incomplete: *Entrance portico* with the barrel vaulted ceiling decorated with exquisite rosettes. The delicate *Cherubs* in the frieze are by Desiderio da Settignano; the cupola decoration is by Luca Della Robbia; the beautiful carved wood door is by Giuliano da Maiano (1472).

**Interior.** Elegant central plan creation; grey stone fluted columns inserted in the white walls, sustain the harmonious cupola. The *Lantern* high *up,* with its graceful small columns, illuminates the barrel vaults. At the sides are crests of the Pazzi family, represented by dolphins. Even the Evangelists in the polychromed medallions are believed to be by Brunelleschi. The beautiful window in the apse with St. Andrew is attributed to Baldovinetti.

Fig. 167

**Fig. 168 - Casa Buonarroti - Façade**     **Fig. 169 - Michelangelo - Self-portrait**

Returning to Piazza Santa Croce, the narrow Via dei Pepi leads to the nearby Via Ghibellina, where, at No. 70, indicated by Michelangelo's bust over the door, is Casa Buonarroti (fig. 168) (the house of Michelangelo Buonarroti).

## CASA BUONARROTI

This is not the house in which Michelangelo was born (he was born in the barren and solitary village of Caprese in Casentino, in the province of Arezzo), but rather the one bought by the artist for his nephew Leonardo Buonarroti. It was decorated by Michelangelo's grand-nephew in the XVII century and was transformed into a Museum in 1859, when it was generously given to the city by his successors. In 1964, during the centenary celebrations, Casa Buonarroti was destined as the seat of the "Michelangelo Study Center". After some restorations the Museum, dedicated exclusively to the great artist, was reopened to the public in 1965.

**Entrance.** *Bronze bust of Michelangelo,* by Daniele da Volterra. In the rooms on the left are some plaster models of the artist's most famous

194

**Figs. 170-171 - Michelangelo: Madonna of the Stairs - Wooden Christ, now in the Church of S. Spirito**

sculptures. In the rooms on the right: self-portrait of Michelangelo (fig. 169). In the following rooms: a small picture-gallery of the Buonarroti family where, among other works, is the celebrated portrait of Vittoria Colonna, perhaps by Pontormo.

**First Floor.** Beginning on the left: *Madonna and Child* called *Madonna of the Stairs* (fig. 170), young work by Michelangelo which was inspired by Donatello's bas-relief; on the right, marble relief of the *Battle of the Centaurs and Lapites,* also from the master's youth (c. 1492). Also displayed are two wax models for the David and a Terra-cotta model for the Madonna and Child in the New Sacristy in San Lorenzo.

In the room on the left are drawings by Michelangelo and a design for the façade of the Church of San Lorenzo. Continuing on the right: apartments of Michelangelo's nephew Leonardo with XVII cent. frescoes representing *Episodes from the life of Michelangelo,* and important *designs* for fortifications. Finally we point out the *torso of a river god* in terra-cotta, intended for the Medici Chapels, left incomplete.

**Second floor.** Reserved for the "Michelangelo Study Centre".

*Piazza of Santissima Annunziata - Portico and Hospital of the Innocents - Church of SS. Annunziata - Etruscan and Egyptian Museums.* (Plan of the Monuments N. 23-24).

## PIAZZA SS. ANNUNZIATA

This is the first Renaissance square with a portico of rounded arches, designed by Brunelleschi. In the center is the bronze *equestrian statue* of Ferdinand I of the Medici, last work by Giambologna, finished by Tacca in 1608. The decoration of the pedestal, with the *queen bee* and an inscription in honor of Ferdinand I, is from 1640. The two graceful *Fountains* in bronze, with fantastic marine monsters, considered among the most important of their kind, are by Tacca and helpers (1629). On the corner of the square and Via dei Servi is the Riccardi Mannelli Palace (with the brick façade) by Ammannati (c. 1577).

## PORTICO OF THE HOSPITAL OF THE INNOCENTS

Begun by Brunelleschi in 1420 (fig. 172), continued and finished with slight variations by Francesco della Luna in 1445.

In the spaces above the nine arches are the famous terra-cotta medallions showing *abbandoned babies in swaddling clothes,* imploring help from their mothers with their innocent gestures, by Andrea Della

Fig. 172 - Square of the SS. Annunziata

Robbia (1486), beloved nephew and pupil of Luca.

The square, left incomplete because of the death of Brunelleschi, was continued in the central portico by Manetti and Antonio da San Gallo, to whom the central arch is attributed, and finished later by Caccini. The portico on the left, by Antonio da San Gallo and Baccio d'Agnolo (1516-25), inspired by Brunelleschi on the opposite side of the square, has the letter "S" in the medallions, referring to the Servite fathers who officiate the Church.

**Hospital of the Innocents.** Founded in 1421 during the Florentine Republic, this was the first instituion of its kind in Europe.

Observe, under the portico on the left, the inscription on the closed window surmounted by two putti that recalls the "ruota" (wheel) and was used until 1875. With this device children were left while their mothers remained anonymous. Through the door in the center of the portico is the entrance to the Hospital for the Innocents, with its beautiful courtyard where, in the lunette over the door, is an *Annunciation* in terra-cotta by Andrea Della Robbia.

On the right is the entrance to the rooms that contain portraits of the benefactors. Farther ahead is a SMALL MUSEUM, with works by Giovanni del Biondo, Neri di Bicci, Piero di Cosimo and others. Also the famous *Adoration* by Domenico Ghirlandaio (1488), who put his self-portrait in the second figure on the right of the Virgin. From Ghirlandaio's school are: the *Slaughter of the Innocents,* the *Stories of Saints,* the *Passion* and *St. Anthony consecrating the Church of this Hospital.*

## CHURCH OF SANTISSIMA ANNUNZIATA

The Church rose on the old Oratory of the Servites of Mary founded in 1235 by seven young nobles who, tired of the fighting between factions, retired here to a life of contemplation. In order to isolate themselves completely from the city, they then founded the Monastery of Monte Senario, beyond Fiesole. In the middle of the XV century Michelozzo built the first Cloister. The Church, begun by Michelozzo (1444) and Pagno Partigiani, was modified later by Alberti, at the expense of the Marquis of Gonzaga.

**First Cloister.** On the walls, the frescoes represent, beginning from right to left: the *Assumption* (1517) by Rosso Fiorentino; the *Visitation* (1516) by Pontormo; *Marriage of the Virgin* (1513) by Franciabigio; *Birth of the Virgin* and the *Adoration of the Magi* by Andrea del Sarto, who portrayed his wife Lucrezia del Fede in the face of the Madonna. After the door, the *Nativity* with its ample landscape by Baldovinetti (1460), badly deteriorated by the weather. Following is *St. Filippo Ben-*

*izzi assuming the Habit of the Order* by Cosimo Rosselli. The other *Scenes of the Miracles of the Saint* are by Andrea del Sarto (buried in the church and remembered here with a marble bust).

**Interior.** It has a single nave with a large cupola, called the "rotunda", built on a design by Alberti. The deep lateral chapels, fancily decorated in the XVIII century, alter Alberti's construction. The beautiful carved and dedorated *ceiling* is by P. Giambelli, following a design by Volterrano (XVII cent.).

Entering on the left one sees the

**Marble Tempietto,** designed by Michelozzo (1448-61). It is closed by an exquisite bronze cord grill. The rich votive lamps were donated by the Medici and other faithful. The XVII century *silver altar* portrays a Medici Prince praying. This small temple (tempietto) was erected to honor the miraculous *Annunciation* frescoed on the wall (fig. 173), that, according to legend, was painted by an angel while the XIV century artist was sleeping, worried that he would not be able to represent the Virgin in such a way as to surpass the beauty of the angel that he had already painted. The face of *Christ* on the pyx is by Andrea del Sarto.

In the Chapels on the left of the nave, among the most important works are: *God the Father with St. Jerome* and *The Trinity* by Andrea del Castagno; farther ahead is the *Assumption* by Perugino. In the chapel to the right of the main altar is a *Tomb* with a *Deposition,* by Bandinelli (1559) who is buried here with his wife. At the right of the entrance to the dome, *Tomb* of Donato dell'Antella, who died in 1666, by Foggini. On the left: *Tomb of Bishop Angelo Marzi Medici,* by Francesco da Sangallo (1546). The small monumental stone on the floor indicates where Andrea del Sarto was buried. The *High Altar,* enclosed by a balustrade, is enriched by a silver ciborium. The fresco of the cupola, representing the *Incoronation of the Virgin,* is by Volterrano (XVII cent.). In the left transept is the

**Chapel of Baptism**, containing a statue of the *Baptist* in terra-cotta by Michelozzo. From this side we enter the corridor that leads around the tribune, where, among the many surrounding Chapels, is the one at the end called "Cappella del Soccorso" (N. 13 of the plan), that Giambologna created for his tomb and those of his collaborators. It is an interesting chapel with a bronze Crucifix and bronze reliefs with *Scenes of the Passion,* all works by Giambologna.

Leaving the church, on the right, is the entrance to the CLOISTER OF THE DEAD built by Portigiani following a design by Michelozzo (XV cent.). It is called "Cloister of the Dead" because at one time great Florentine families were buried here, as shown by the numerous mon-

**Fig. 173 - Miraculous Image of the SS. Annunziata (Unknown Tuscan Artist - XIV cent.)**

**Fig. 174 - Etruscan Museum - The Chimera, bronze**

umental slabs. In the lunettes: *Stories of the Servites of Mary* by Poccetti, Matteo Rosselli and other XVII cent. artists. In the lunette above the door of the church (under glass), is the famous *Madonna del Sacco,* by Andrea del Sarto (1525). In the corner on the left is the door leading to the *Chapel of St. Luke* (generally closed). Under the chapel are buried Cellini, Pontormo, Franciabigio, Bartolini and other artists. Perugino was buried in the church but the exact place is not known. (The church does not have an appropriate bell-tower).

Returning to the square, on the left is the **Archaeological Museum.** Because of the serious damage caused by the flood, the rooms on the ground floor are still in restoration. The building in which the museum is located is called "of the crocetta" because it is in the form of a cross. The entrance is on Via della Colonna past the garden, enclosed by the fence. This Museum is considered one of the most important in the world for Etruscan art and sculture. Among the most important works we mention: in the large rooms of the first floor, the *Chimera* from Arezzo (fig. 174) in bronze (V cent. BC); the "Oratore" (haranguer) (III-II cent. BC); "Idolino", bronze Greek sculpure (second half V cent.). Among the numerous works is the famous *Françoise Vase* of ancient Greek origin.

In the rooms of the first floor, on the left, is the very important *Egyptian Museum.*

# SIXTH ITINERARY

*Church of S. Maria Novella - Via dei Fossi - Piazza Goldoni - Via della Vigna Nuova - Palazzo Rucellai - Church of Ognissanti - Lungarno and Vespucci Bridge - Alla Carraia Bridge - Lungarno and Corsini Palace - Bridge and Church of St. Trinita - Church of SS. Apostoli - Palace of the Guelph Party - Davanzati Palace - Strozzi Palace* (Map of the monuments nos. 1, 27, 28, 30, 31, 32 and 33).

## CHURCH OF SANTA MARIA NOVELLA

It was begun in 1278 by the Dominican Friars Sisto and Ristoro and was finished in 1360. The beautiful bell-tower is by Fra Jacopo Talenti and helpers in Lombard style with several stories decorated with small arches and harmonious mullioned windows.

**Façade** (fig. 175). The façade was built around 1300 with green and white marble and harmonizes well with the architectural complex of the Church. While the lower part is in Gothic style with Romanesque traces (the blind arches were inspired by the Baptistry), the beautiful *portal* and upper part were designed by Alberti (1456) in the Renaissance pe-

Fig. 175 - Square and Church of Santa Maria Novella

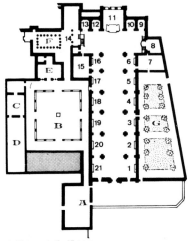

riod. The two *astronomical instruments* at the right and left are by Ignazio Danti (1512), the Court Astronomer of Cosimo I. On the right side is the old *Cemetery* of the noble families (enclosed by the portico) that givens its name to the small street (Via degli Avelli).

**Interior.** It is in the form of a "T" with a nave, two aisles, and cross valuted ceiling. The length is 99 meters, width 28 meters and width of the transept 61 meters. In the centre *Crucifix* by Giotto.

The clustered columns are more closely spaced at the front, creating an enhanced perspective effect. Fortunately the Church did not suffer the unfortunate alterations of Santa Croce: here Vasari limited himself to modifying the center of the nave and adding the lateral altars. Among the most notable works we mention, at the beginning of the right: *Monument to the Blessed Villana,* by Bernardo Rossellini and helpers (1415).

Observe, on a pillar of the nave, to the left: *Pulpit* with spiral staircase, by Buggiano, following a design by Brunelleschi, with low-reliefs representing *Stories of the Virgin between gilded frames and laurel garlands inspired by Trajan's column in Rome.*

Behind the pulpit, on the wall of the left aisle, a fresco (restored) by Masaccio (1427) showing *The Trinity with Mary and St. John;* below the portraits of the donors kneeling. In false high relief there is a skeleton (Death) with an iscription which reads: "As thou art now so once was I: As I am now so will thou be".

**High Altar.** The beautiful stained glass windows are of the XV cent. The altar of polychrome marble (added in the XIX cent.) alters the atmospere and has a *candelabrum* of the XV century. If there is no religious service the apse is the best viewpoint for the famous frescoes in which Domenico Ghirlandaio (1485-90), aided by his many collaborators and students, among whom was young Michelangelo, painted the most faithful documentation of the private life of the wealthy XV century Florentine society. In the *Scenes of the Virgin and St. John the Baptist* (fig. 176) *women and girls* are shown with their typical headdresses and many famous *Florentine personages* are represented in the costumes of the time. On the lower central wall is a portrait of the donor *Giovanni Tornabuoni* and his *wife Francesca Pitti.*

In the vault are *large figures of the Evangelists.* Following, on the right, is the STROZZI CHAPEL with frescoes by Filippino Lippi (1502), representing the *Miracles of the Apostles Philip and John.* Behind the altar, *tomb of Filippo Strozzi,* a masterpiece by Benedetto da Maiano (1491-93). Observe, on the wall in front of this Chapel, among other works, terra-cotta bust of *St. Antonino,* of the XV cent. Above is the *Gothic tomb of Todice Aliotti,* Bishop of Fiesole, who died in 1436, by Tino da Camaino. Below, on the left, *Tomb of Joseph, Patriarch of Costantinople,* who died in this convent during the Council of Florence of

**Fig. 176 - St. Maria Novella - Main Chapel - Domenico Ghirlandaio: Scenes of the Madonna**

**Fig. 177 - Basilica of St. Maria Novella - Spanish Chapel - Andrea da Firenze: Central and right walls**

1439, that unified the Greek and Roman Churches. Ending the transept is the raised RUCELLAI CHAPEL with XIV cent. frescoes. In the floor is the *memorial figure of the Domenican Leonardo Dati,* by Ghiberti (1452), at one time in front of the main altar. On the left: BARDI CHAPEL or of the *Sacrament* with XIV cent. frescoes attributed by Longhi to the Bolognese painter Lippo Dalmasio. Returning to the *transept,* on the left is the GONDI CHAPEL built by Giuliano da Sangallo (1503) in polychrome marble. On the altar is the celebrated *Crucifix* by Brunelleschi. In the vault, the deteriorated frescoes were perhaps done by Greek artists who worked in Florence in the XIII century.

GADDI CHAPEL. Architectural decoration by Giovanni Antonio Dosio (1575-77); in the vault, frescoes and stuccoes by Alessandro Allori. On the altar is a tablet by Bronzino, *Jesus resuscitating the daughter of Jairus.*

From here one steps up to the CHAPEL OF THE STROZZI OF MANTUA, entirely frescoed by Nardo di Cione (XIV cent.). On the back wall, the *Last Judgement;* on the left, *Paradise* inspired by Dante's Divine Comedy, who is represented among the *elect.* On the right wall, the *Circles of Hell.* On the altar, the altar-piece, signed and dated 1357, is by Andrea di Cione called Orcagna, Nardo's brother. At the foot of the stairs, on the right we enter the beautiful *Sacristy* by Fra Jacopo Talenti (1350), the architect of the bell-tower. It contains the beautiful *lavabo* of marble and glazed terra-cotta by Giovanni Della Robbia, above is a *wooden Crucifix.* The large wardrobes are of the XVII century. Heading towards the exit, observe, in the end wall of the Church, the large stained glass *rose-window* with the *Incoronation of the Virgin,* believed to be designed by Botticelli, as is the mosaic *Nativity* in the lunette.

Below, on the right wall, *Annunciation, Nativity, Epiphany* and *Baptism,* XIV century Florentine frescoes. Leaving the church, on the right is the entrance to the

**Green Cloister** (Chiostro Verde). So-called because of the colors of the famous frescoes on the walls. They represent: *Scenes from the Old Testament,* among which we mention the *Deluge* and the *Drunkenness of Noah,* by Paolo Uccello who was the first artist seriously to study the laws of volumetric movement in perspective. Under the portico, opposite the entrance on the left, a beautiful portal, flanked by two wide mullioned windows with twisted columns, leads to the famous SPANISH CHAPEL (fig. 177).

# SPANISH CHAPEL

A splendid architectural creation of Jacopo Talenti (c. 1350), it served as the Chapter House of the Convent, later for the religious functions of the Spanish members at the court of Eleanor of Toledo, wife of Cosimo I. On the walls and in the vault of this splendid Chapel, we can admire the famous cycle of frescoes by Andrea Bonaiuti, called da Firenze (c. 1355) representing the allegorical theme of *True Penitence,* taken from a poem by Passavanti (1298-1358). On the left wall, *Triumph of St. Thomas Aquinas.* On the right wall: *Activity and Triumph of the Dominicans:* on the left, the *civil authorities dominating mortals;* in the background is the *cupola of the Cathedral,* as imagined by the XIV cent. artist. Observe on the right wall *the black and white dogs (Domini canes-hounds of God) who defend the flock of Cristians from the wolves (heretics).* Above: *St. Dominic, St. Thomas and St. Peter Martyr confuting the heretics.* Youth is represented by *Ladies and Knights who waste their lives in worldly pastimes*; a *Dominican* confesses and absolves a *penitent.* Still higher, *St. Dominic indicates the way tp Paradise, St. Peter wellcomes the faithful who are crowned by two angels.* At the top of the Chapel is a *Christ in glory.*

Returning to the Cloister, farther ahead on the left, is a SECOND SMALL CLOISTER. At one time it was the cemetery of the great families, with XIV century frescoes and a *Noli me tangere* in terra-cotta, by Della Robbia.

Returning to the square observe the two marble obelisks, with four bronze tortoises at the base by Giambologna (1608). The obelisks served as markers during the "Palio" races that were held here from 1563. On the opposite side of the square is the LOGGIA OF SAN PAOLO (1489-96), inspired by Brunelleschi's portico in Piazza SS. Annunziata. On the front are nine terracotta medallions by Giovanni, the last of the Della Robbia. In the first medallion on the left is a *self-portrait of Andrea Della Robbia* who portrayed his uncle Luca on the extreme right. In the lunette under the portico, *Meeting of St. Francis and St. Dominic in Rome,* a masterpiece by Andrea Della Robbia. On the corner of Via della Scala, *Tabernacle with Madonna and Saints,* by Francesco d'Antonio replaced by a copy (c. 1425). Walking around the square, on the side of the Via delle Belle Donne, one can better admire the Church which Michelangelo used to call "my bride". Returning to the portico of San Paolo is the Via dei Fossi, on which are many antique shops, leading to Piazzetta Goldoni, with a *statue of the venetian poet* by Cambi (1873). On the left is Via Vigna Nuova where, at N. 18, we can admire the beautiful *Rucellai Palace.*

**Rucellai Palace.** Built to plans by Leon Battista Alberti who, inspired by antiquity, is stylistically opposite to Brunelleschi. Observe the exquisite pilasters of the Doric, Ionic and Corinthian orders and the slightly rusticated ashlars which render the façade harmonious and linear, rather than plastic. The beautiful two-light windows are of a traditional character. The Museum of "The History of Photography" from the ancient Casa Alinari is situated on the ground floor. Opposite the palace is the *Loggia Rucellai* attributed to Alberti, that has been brought back to its original aspect after having been walled up in the XVII century.

Returning to Piazzetta Goldoni we continue along Borgo Ognissanti where, farther ahead, lies the Hospital of St. Giovanni di Dio, which occupies the old Vespucci houses where Amerigo Vespucci was born. (He is buried in Avila, Spain).

## PIAZZA OGNISSANTI

Facing the square are two large hotels, the Excelsior and the Grand Hotel. In the center, the modern bronze group of *Hercules fighting the Lion* is by Romano Romanelli. On the corner of Borgognissanti, Lensi Busini Palace (later Quaratesi), with XV century graffiti and overhanging upper floors, now seat of the French Institute.

## CHURCH OF OGNISSANTI (ALL SAINTS)

Founded in the XIII century, it was entirely reconstructed in the XVIII century. Above the door, the lunette in glazed terra-cotta showing the *Incoronation of the Virgin* is attributed to Benedetto Buglioni. The beautiful Romanesque bell-tower is of the XIII cent.

**Interior.** Seventeenth century style with a single nave and a transept. Beginning on the right wall: the second altar, frescoes by Domenico and David Ghirlandaio (c. 1470); above, *Madonna of Mercy who gathers the Vespucci family under her mantle.*

Ahead, between the third and fourth altars, *St. Augustine in his Study,* fresco by Botticelli (1480). Followed by a XVI century *pulpit* with marble bas-reliefs of *Stories of St. Francis.*

Turning into the right transept and entering the chapel on the right, we see on the floor the marble disc marking the spot where Botticelli was buried.

Fig. 178

**Fig. 178 - Refectory of Ognissanti - Domenico Ghirlandaio: Last Supper**

**High Altar.** In the cupola, *Glory of Paradise,* fresco by Giovanni da San Giovanni (1616-17). Heading towards the door notice on the wall between the fourth and third altars, *St. Jerome in his study* by Domenico Ghirlandaio (1480); it is interesting to compare it with Botticelli's on the opposite wall, which is psychologically more vibrant. Leaving the Church, on the right, you may visit the picturesque Cloister of the Convent, in the style of Michelozzo, with frescoes by Florentine artists of the XVII century. In the back, to the left, is the entrance to the Refectory with Domenico Ghirlandaio's *Last Supper* (1480) which was admired by Leonardo (fig. 178). Proceeding to the river, on the right, notice the

**Vespucci Bridge.** Built after the last war with contributions from the Latin American Nations. Continuing along the Arno we can admire the scenery offered by the hillside of Bellosguardo and the cupola of the Seminary of Cestello in front of us. In the distance Michelangelo Square and San Miniato. Walking left on Lungarno we reach Ponte alla Carraia, destroyed by the German mines (1944) rebuilt in its original style.
After the bridge begins Lungarno Corsini; on the corner of Piazzetta Goldoni is the RICASOLI PALACE, attributed to Michelozzo. Ahead is the CORSINI PALACE, by Silvani and Antonio Ferri (XVII cent.), with the beautiful courtyard and lateral wings that, because of its rational elegance, inspired other residential palaces in Europe. On the first floor of the Palace is the *Art Gallery,* considered one of the most important private Galleries and containing works by Signorelli, Raphael and other famous artists. For the visit consult the door-man. On the ground floor is the seat of the cultural society "Leonardo da Vinci". The Corsini family had some important historical figures among its members, like Andrea, bishop of Fiesole (XIV cent.), and Lorenzo later Pope Clement XII. Farther ahead an epigraph marks the site of the houses of the Compagni, the family to which the historian Dino Compagni, contemporary of Dante, belonged. At N° 4 is PALAZZO GIANFIGLIAZZI, a Renaissance building modified in the last century; an inscription records that Manzoni stayed here in 1872. At N° 2 another tablet marks where Vittorio Alfieri died in 1803.

**Santa Trinita Bridge** (fig. 179). This jewel of Italian architecture by Ammannati (1570), consists of three wide arches sustained by enormous pillars. Destroyed in the last war, it was rebuilt by the Florentines exactly as it had been and where it had been, using the original stones recovered from the river. The four statues that decorate the corners are *Summer* and *Autumn* by Caccini, *Winter* by Landini, and *Spring* by Francavilla. These statues fell into the river because of the mine explosions

**Figs. 179-180 - Bridge of Santa Trinita and Square of Santa Trinita**

**Fig. 180 bis - Basilica of Santa Trinita - Domenico Ghirlandaio: St. Francis resuscitates a child**

but were recovered and put back in their original positions. The head of Spring was still missing and an American newspaper offered a generous reward for its finding. In 1961, during some works in the river, the head was found by a town employee, much to the joy of the Florentines who had given it up for lost or stolen during the war.

On the left of the bridge is the SPINI-FERRONI PALACE (1298), perfect example of a typical wealthy medieval home, three stories high with a crenellated top.

## PIAZZA SANTA TRINITA

In the small square (fig. 180), the tall *granite column* originally at the Baths of Caracalla, was donated by Pius IV to Cosimo I, who had it placed here to commemorate the victory of Montemurlo (1537). The porphyry statue of "Justice" on the top of the column is by Tadda (1581). The bronze mantle was added later. On the right of the square, is the beautiful BARTOLINI-SALIMBENI PALACE by Baccio d'Agnolo, who with this palace began a new style of homes for the rich. The criticism of his fellow citizens prompted him to engrave over the door: "carpere promptius quam imitari", that is, "to criticize is easier than to imitate".

# CHURCH OF SANTA TRINITA

Considered one of the oldest churches of the city, it is in Florentine Gothic style. Built by the Vallombrosian monks in the XI cent., it was rebuilt in the XII cent. and enlarged in the following century. The late Renaissance façade is by Buontalenti (1593-94). The statue of *St. Alexis* on the left, and the relief on the central door representing the *Trinity* are by Caccini.

**Interior.** The church has a nave and two aisles with pointed arches and cross vaults. The chapels were added in the XIV century. On the interior façade can be seen remains of the original Romanesque church; the fresco of the *Trinity* is of the late XIV century.

Among the important works we mention: the fourth chapel of the right aisle (Bartolini Chapel), frescoed by the late-Gothic painter Lorenzo Monaco (teacher of Beato Angelico), who represented *Stories of Mary* and *figures of the Prophets* in the vault; on the altar the *Annunciation.* In the right transept, on the tall column, *statue of David;* in the lunette, *Sibilla Tiburtina announces the birth of the Saviour to Augustus,* by Domenico Ghirlandaio (1483). By the same artist we admire in the Sassetti Chapel *Stories and miracles of St. Francis* (fig. 181), among these: *St. Francis resuscitates a child* (fig. 180 bis); above, portrait of *Politian* with *Lorenzo the Magnificent and his children* shown in a typical Florentine background with the personages wearing costumes and head-dresses of the times. In the frescoes we can see the *Spini Palace, Ponte St. Trinità* and the *Loggia in Signoria Square.* Below, on the sides, *Tombs of Francesco Sassetti and his wife Nera Corsi,* the donors of the *Chapel,* shown in prayer. On the altar, *Adoration of the Shepherds,* also by Ghirlandaio, inspired by the "Triptych" of Hugo Van der Goes in the Uffizi Gallery. The following Chapel contains the miraculous *Crucifixion, called of St. Giovanni Gualberto* (generally covered), founder of the Vallombrosian order (XI cent.). According to legend, this Crucified Figure bent its head in a sign of approval because St. Giovanni pardoned his brother's murderer.

**High Altar.** On the altar is a triptych with *Trinity and Saints* by Mariotto di Nardo (1416). In the vault and in the lunettes, the frescoes (unfortunately deteriorated) are by Alessio Baldovinetti (c. 1471), with the *Patriarchs, Sacrifice of Isaac* and *Moses receiving the tablets of the law.* In the second chapel (on the left of the High Altar), famous *tomb of Bishop Benozzo Federighi,* rare marble sculpture by Luca Della Robbia (1454-56), with a frieze in polychrome terracotta. In the fifth chapel of the left aisle, *wooden statue* of *Mary Magdalen* by Desiderio da Settignano and Benedetto da Maiano, inspired, it is believed, by Donatello's

Magdalen. In the central nave, the stairs lead down to the *Romanesque Crypt,* that conserves some elements of the primitive church. Returning to the Piazza St. Trinità, observe the elegant via Tornabuoni, known for its famous palaces, its book stores and elegant shops. The first circle of walls around Florence passed here and continued on Borgo SS. Apostoli out to the Ponte Vecchio. The brief walk on the right, gives us a chance to admire one of the sections of the city that best conserves its old aspect and leads us to the Church of SS. Apostoli.

## CHURCH OF SS. APOSTOLI

The Church (generally opened in the morning) was built in the XI century but was remodelled in the XV and XVI centuries. After some opportune restorations it has once again acquired its original aspect. The beautiful *Portal* is attributed to Bendetto da Rovezzano.

*Interior.* The interior has a nave and two aisles divided by columns, with a semicircular apse. It is a splendid example of Florentine-Romanesque architecture, like the Baptistry and San Miniato. The classic proportions of this church certainly influenced the Renaissance building designed by Brunelleschi. In the Church are conserved some stone splinters from the Holy Sepulchre which are used as a flint to light the fire-works in the XVIII century cart during the "Scoppio del Carro" on Easter Sunday, in front of the Baptistry. On the left of the apse, terra-cotta *tabernacle* by Giovanni Della Robbia, and *Tomb of Oddo Altoviti* by Benedetto da Rovezzano. Leaving the Church, farther ahead, observe the Medieval "tower-houses". On the right "Roselli Del Turco Palace" by Baccio d'Agnolo (early XVI cent.). On the left is the narrow via del Fiordaliso, with interesting medieval houses whose upper stories jut out supported on corbels.

Continuing on Borgo SS. Apostoli, at $N^o$ 8, on the left, remains of the houses of the Buondelmonti, which were destroyed in the "Ciompi" riots in 1378. The remains were included in the building of the Carthusian monks. According to Legend, the origins of the struggles between Guelphs and Ghibellines in Florence, begin with the slaying of Buondelmonte dei Buondelmonti (Easter 1215). Farther ahead is the central via Por Santa Maria. On the left, via delle Terme with its old tower-houses. Nearby the building of the "Borsa Merci" (Stock market) was built after the last war, but it unfortunately covers the old palace of the "Guelph Party". On the left of the Palace of Guelph Party is the small, narrow Via del Capaccio, with its beautiful XV cent. Canacci Palace with graffiti decoration and its splendid loggia.

On the right is the Palazzo dei Capitani di Parte Guelfa.

IHESVM QVEM GENVIT ADORAVIT MARIA

Fig. 141

## PALAZZO DEI CAPITANI DI PARTE GUELFA

Splendid XIV cent. building with wide mullioned windows, decorated with crests below the embattlements. The picturesque covered staircase with small octagonal columns leads to the first floor, where Brunelleschi built the large Renaissance hall with smooth walls and large windows, that faces Via delle Terme and Via Capaccio. The staircase on Via Capaccio was added by Vasari. In the large hall with the beautiful wooden ceiling, enriched by works by Luca Della Robbia, cultural conferences and political meetings are held. On the left of the open stairs is the ex church of San Biagio, now the seat of the "Università Popolare" (University of the People), with its famous Library.

Continuing on the left, on Via Porta Rossa, we come to the medieval Piazza Davanzati with its cut down tower-house. On the left is the Davizzi-Davanzati Palace.

## DAVIZZI-DAVANZATI PALACE

Of the XIV cent. with the "Loggia" added in the XV century, it is now a Museum. A visit is particularly recommended since it is the only example of a XV cent. Florentine-home, reorganized with furniture copied from the originals now in the Museum of Philadelphia. From here we can admire the old Torrigiani Palace of the XIV Century (now the Hotel Porta Rossa). Continuing on the right, in Piazza Davanzati behind the Central Post Office, is Via Sassetti where the remains of some old palaces can be seen. On the left is Piazza Strozzi with the Odeon Cinema, which is located in the "Strozzino", begun by Michelozzo (1458), continued by Giuliano da Sangallo (1460-65). On the right is the Strozzi Palace.

## STROZZI PALACE

Begun by Benedetto da Maiano (fig. 182), for Filippo Strozzi, an unfortunate rival of the Medici. It is a splendid example of civil architecture with its rusticated stone, inspired by the Medici-Riccardi Palace, but with more harmonious proportions. The *palace* has beautiful mullioned windows and a magnificent cornice, typical of the Florentine palaces of the time, left incomplete by Cronaca, who continued the construction of the palace until 1507. Also by Cronaca is the beautiful courtyard, inspired by Michelozzo. The famous wrought-iron lanterns that decorate the corners of the palace exterior, are by the bizarre and able artisan, Caparra. To-day the palace is used for international expositions like the biennial Antique Show, and other cultural and artistic manifestations and the biennial "Aurea" exhibition of goldsmiths' work. Here also is the seat of the "Center of Renaissance Studies" and the noted "Gabinetto Vieusseux", with the Library and reading-room.

**Fig. 182 - Strozzi Palace**

# FIRST EXCURSION

*Viale dei Colli* (Avenue of the Hills) - *Piazzale Michelangelo - Church of San Miniato* (South of the city - Monumental plan Nos. 24 and 35 - Bus N: 13).

These winding avenues that are a continuation of those surrounding the city below, are called "of the hills", because they were built on the green picturesque hillside by the Florentine Architect Giuseppe Poggi.

## PIAZZALE MICHELANGELO

This is renowned as one of the most panoramic sites of Italy (fig. 183). Superb is the view of the city and the hills of Fiesole enjoyed from this spot. Looking down we can admire the various bridges and the Arno which flows towards Pisa, flanked in the distance by the famous Cascine Park. To the left of the Piazzale, are the picturesque walls of San Giorgio and the Belvedere Fortress. Standing with one's back to the city, to the left of the Square, high up, is the Church of San Miniato; on the right in the distance, the Castle of *Torre del Gallo.* In the center of the Piazzale is a bronze copy of Michelangelo's *David* and bronze copies of his statues of *Night, Day, Dusk* and *Dawn,* the originals of which are in the Medici Chapels. Moving towards the left at the end of the square, observe the picturesque stairs, called "Monte alle Croci" (Hill of the Crosses) because of the symbolic stations of the Cross, that lead to the Franciscan *Church of S. Salvatore al Monte,* rebuilt in the XVI century following a design by Cronaca. Higher up, to the right, is the *Church of San Miniato al Monte.*

## CHURCH OF SAN MINIATO AL MONTE

The church is inserted between the beautiful Bishop's Palace (1296-1320) (now inhabited by the monks of Monte Oliveto) on the right, and, on the left, the remains of the old bastions, with the *bell-Tower* by Baccio d'Agnolo damaged during the famous siege of 1530, which saw Michelangelo as the engineer of the Florentine fortifications. The façade of the Church is strictly Florentine Romanesque style with green and white marble. In the tympanum is a XII cent. mosaic representing *Christ between the Madonna and San Miniato* (fig. 185). The Church (fig. 184), was built in the XI century on the old Oratory (erected by San Miniato, the first Florentine Christian martyr), and is the most notable example of Florentine Romanesque architecture.

Fig. 183 - Piazzale Michelangelo - View of the city
Fig. 184 - Basilica of San Miniato al Monte

Fig. 185 - Basilica of San Miniato - Christ blessing (mosaic)

**Interior** (fig. 186). A nave and two aisles. The wall structure is intact but the decorative part has been restored (the roof, columns and lateral walls). The beautiful floor of the central nave is richly decorated with inlaid marble Signs of the Zodiac, among which are lions, doves and other symbols (1207). In the center of the Church is the small but splendid marble Renaissance Chapel by Michelozzo (1442) built to house the *Crucifixion of St. Giovanni Gualberto* (now conserved in the Church of St. Trinità). The altar-piece by Agnolo Gaddi represent *Episodes of Saint Miniato, St. Giovanni Gualberto,* the *Annunciation* and *Stories of the Passion.* The Chapel is enriched by small Corinthian columns and pilasters, and the barrel vaulted roof decorated in terra-cotta by Luca Della Robbia, with the motto "Semper" by the donor, Piero dei Medici.

**Right aisle.** Old frescoes; among the most notable, *Madonna and Saints* by Paolo Schiavo (1439). In the Crypt, with a cross-vaulted ceiling sustained by slender columns, are the remains of San Miniato.

**Chancel.** Raised and enclosed by a splendid balustrade decorated with inlaid green and white marble rosettes. The famous *pulpit* (1207) is the most notable work of XIII century Florentine sculpture. The exquisite inlaid wood stalls are by Giovanni da Gaiole and Francesco di Dom-

Fig. 186 - Basilica of San Miniato - Interior - Michelozzo and L. Della Robbia: Tabernacle

enico (1470). Farther ahead on the right, is the Sacristy with frescoes by Spinello Aretino (1387) showing *Stories and Miracles of St. Benedict.*

From the chancel observe the semi-circular apse, with arches and columns of black and white marble and graceful capitals; the large mosaic (1279) (restored) with *Christ between the Madonna and St. Miniato crowned* (because he was of Imperial origin). At the base of the mosaic are symbols of the Evangelists. If one is here during the morning when the sun's rays penetrate the windows of the apse, closed with translucent marble slabs, one can see how the soft light discretely illuminates the Church. By ringing the bell at the door it is possible to visit the beautiful cloister and the splendid hall of the Bishop's Palace. Descending once again to the church, on the right is the Chapel of the Cardinal of Portugal.

**Chapel of the Cardinal of Portugal.** The Chapel was built by Antonio Manetti, pupil of Brunelleschi (1459-66), for Jacopo di Lusitania, Archbishop of Lisbon, nephew of King Alfonso of Portugal, and is a strictly Renaissance work. In the vault are five *medallions* by Luca Della Robbia representing the *Holy Spirit* and the *Cardinal Virtues* (1416-66). Against the right wall is the famous *Tomb* of the *Cardinal of Portugal,* masterpiece by Antonio Rossellino. On the altar, the painting of *St. Vincent, St. James* and *St. Eustachius* is a copy of the original by Antonio and Piero Pollaiolo, now in the Uffizi. On the left, *Bishop's chair,* and above, *Annunciation* frescoed by Baldovinetti (1466-67). The two *Flying Angels* are by Antonio del Pollaiolo.

Heading towards the exit, on the right is the *Porta Santa* (Holy Door) so-called because, according to legend, remains of Christian martyrs were found here; on the left is the Tomb of Giuseppe Giusti. Returning to the square in front of the church, we see the Monumental Cemetery.

**Monumental Cemetery.** Called of the "Porte Sante", designed by the architect Matas (1839), where many famous persons are buried including Carlo Lorenzini (Collodi), Stibbert, Temple-Leader, Villari, Salvemini, Giovanni Papini, Eugenio Montale and others.

## SECOND EXCURSION

**San Domenico - Fiesole.** (North of the city. Monumental map N. 38 and 39. Bus service N. 7 from Piazza San Marco. About 6 km. from the center of Florence. Altitude 320 meters).

For those using private cars the usual route goes from Piazza del Duomo to Piazza Libertà. In this square is one of the oldest gates of the city: *Porta S. Gallo* (1284 - plan N. 36). In front of this, the Baroque arch is by Jadod (1745) and was erected for the entrance into Florence of Francesco of Lorraine, the successor of the Medici. Turning right on Viale Matteotti we reach the *English Protestant Cemetery* (plan N. 37) where, among others, the poet Arthur Hugh Clough (d. 1861) and Elisabeth Barret Browing (d. 1863), are buried. Following the signs for Fiesole, we cross a bridge over the railroad and take the third street on the right, Viale Alessandro Volta which leads to the picturesque section called San Domenico which takes its name from the convent (fig. 187).

### CONVENT OF SAN DOMENICO

Built in the XV century. Here the twenty year old Beato Angelico became a Dominican monk. The Church was remodelled in the XVII century by Nigetti and contains, among other interesting works, a *Mad-*

**Fig. 187 - Hills of Fiesole**

*onna and Child with Saints* by Angelico (in the second chapel). There are numerous historical villas in San Domenico, including the "Villa Sparta", on the right of the convent; farther up, surrounded by cypress trees, the "Villa Papiniano"; at the top in a dominating position, painted yellow, is the "Medici Villa" that was a cultural center under Lorenzo the Magnificent. After San Domenico, on the right, the road winds higher between villas with beautiful gardens, olive groves and tall cypresses, making this a landscape of great harmony between nature and man made works.

The high hill on the right is Monte Ceceri, from where Leonardo tried out his first experimental flights. At the last curve near Fiesole is the entrance to the Medici Villa with its splendid park. On the right side are remains of the Etruscan walls.

## FIESOLE

An old Etruscan city, it held a notable position during the Roman era, especially under the Empire. The archaeological zone mentioned later is testimony to the importance of this old city. In Mino da Fiesole Square (fig. 188) is the Cathedral. On the left of the Archbishop's

**Fig. 188 - Fiesole - Piazza Mino and Cathedral**

Palace is the large Seminary. On the right of the Square the bronze equestrian monument of *Vittorio Emanuele II* and *Garibaldi* are by Calzolari (1906), recalling their meeting at Teano.

Behind is the old Municipal building (restored), with crests of the mayors. On the right, *Church of St. Maria Primerana* with its XVII century façade.

**Cathedral**, dedicated to St. Romulus. It was begun in 1028 and covered with the local stone.

**Interior** is Romanesque, divided into a nave and two aisles, with arches sustained by solid stone columns and splendid capitals. As in S. Miniato, here the chancel is raised and, in the first chapel on the right, is the famous *Tomb of Bishop Salutati* by Mino da Fiesole (1466), who sculpted the *bust of the Bishop,* one of his most vibrant works. In the next chapel is an old copy of the *Martyrdom of St. Romulus* in which we see Fiesole as it was at the time. On the *High Altar,* the triptych with the *Madonna, Child and Saints* is by Bicci di Lorenzo (1440). In the apse are XVI cent. frescoes with *Stories of St. Romulus.* In the church observe the XV cent. pulpit that inspired Brunelleschi for the one in Santa Maria Novella. Returning to the square behind the apse of the Cathedral is the entrance to the Roman Theatre.

## ROMAN THEATRE AND ARCHAEOLOGICAL ZONE

After admiring the solemn scenery that encloses such great testimony of the past, on the right we enter the *Tempietto,* in Ionic style, by Ezio Cerpi (1912-14), which is a small Museum containing archaeological objects found in the Fiesole area. Among these is the statuette of Etruscan-Ionic art representing *Hercules* (VI cent. BC); the Etruscan mirror with the *Sacrifice of Polixena,* the head of the statue of Claudius. Leaving the Museum, below right is the Roman Theatre (fig. 189).

**Roman Theatre.** In Greek style, the Theatre was discovered in 1809 and excavated by Gamurrini (1873). It dates back to Silla, was enriched in the I and II centuries A.D., and was enlarged during Hadrian's era. Heading down towards the west, we see two sacrificial altars from Etruscan times. On the left is an Etrusco-Roman Temple, of which the entrance steps are conserved. On the right of the Temple the remains of an Etruscan gate are visible, with parts of the Etruscan wall, built with colossal blocks, that extends eastwards to the Baths. Leaving the Roman Theatre, on the right is the

**Fig. 189 - Fiesole - Roman Theater**

## BANDINI MUSEUM

On the ground floor are some terra-cotta works; on the first floor in the first room, works by Bicci di Lorenzo, Agnolo and Taddeo Gaddi and other artists identified in the pamphlets available to the visitors. In the second room we can admire works by Botticelli, Filippo Lippi, the famous *Triumphs of Religion, Love Chastity* and *Time,* by Jacopo del Sellaio. After visiting this small but important Museum, if one has time, we suggest walking down to the left on the picturesque road bordered by cypress trees that, winding upward, reaches the *Franciscan Monastery,* passing by the *Monumental Cemetery* where the sculptor Duprè (d. 1882) is buried. Here is this artist's famous *Deposition.* If your time is limited, then return to the main square (Mino da Fiesole), from where you can go straight up Via S. Francesco, located between the *Seminary* and the *Bishop's Palace.* Continuing, up to the right, is the entrance to the small Park from where we can admire the Archaeological Zone below and the surrounding hills.

Leaving the park, on the left, we enter the beautiful panoramic garden, in which there is a *Monument to the War Dead* and a splendid view of the city. From here we arrive at the vast panoramic terrace where, the Etruscan walls were rediscovered. Opposite, in the beautiful square where the panorama is more ample, is the Basilica of St. Alexander, Bishop of the city. This V century church was erected on an Etruscan temple and was renovated and restored in later times. Higher up, we visit the Convent of San Francesco (figs. 190-91).


## CONVENT OF SAN FRANCESCO

In 1330 it was the Oratory of the "Romite Fiorentine". In 1407, the Monastery passed to the Franciscans, who enlarged it in the following eras. The graceful Church has a simple vault. Among the most importants works, behind the beautiful grating, *Annunciation* attributed to Raffaellino del Garbo. The *inlaid stalls* of the choir are of the XV cent., the Renaissance arch is attributed to Benedetto da Maiano. On the left, is the entrance to the Sacristy.

**Sacristy.** Modernized and has frescoes by Baccio M. Bacci. From the graceful *Cloister* we descend to the MISSION MUSEUM. From the balconies we can admire a panorama of Florence, the Cascine Park, which appears as a dark strip, and the Arno which flows towards Pisa. Leaving the Convent, on the left is the entrance to the picturesque MEDIEVAL CLOISTER. The small stair-case leads to the severe cells of the Monastery, where St. Bernardino of Siena lived when he was the Superior of the convent. If the visitor happens to be here at dusk, he will never forget the vast view of Florence, surrounded by her splendid hills.

Returning to the square, the bus leaves for the city. If one has a car, when arriving at S. Domenico, we suggest taking Via Boccaccio on the right, where, after the narrow curves, on the right is the Villa Schifanoia with its graceful garden. It was donated by Myron Taylor to the Vatican (where he was ambassador), and is now the seat of the Pius XII Institute, directed by American Sisters, and frequented by girls studyng music, humanities, fine arts and Italian. Ahead, on the left, is the vast splendid garden of the Villa Palmieri where Boccaccio, taking refuge here from the plague of 1348, is said to have written his Decameron. This historic villa, that hosted Queen Victoria of England in 1888 and famous writers, is now owned by the Committee for the conservation of historic villas.

**Figs. 190-191 - Fiesole - St. Francis - The Church**

## Less frequented Museums, that merit being visited.

**Bardini Museum.** Located on the right of Ponte alle Grazie, in Piazza dei Mozzi (monumental plan N. 20), in front of the XVI century Palace of the Torrigiani, by Baccio d'Agnolo. The XIX century Palace, willed to the city in 1923 with all its art treasures by the antique dealer Bardini, contains, in the large rooms of its two stories, a beautiful *Venetian ceiling,* paintings, tapestries, ceramics and other numerous objects of art.

**Museum of the "Horne Foundation".** This is located on Via dei Benci (near S. Croce) on the right of the picturesque Piazza delle Colonnine, so-called because of the small *loggia* supported by two columns of the Alberti tower-house. It was donated in 1916 to the city of Florence by the writer and collector Herbert P. Horne. The building, formerly of the Alberti then of the Corsi families, is attributed to Giuliano da Sangallo, who executed the beautiful *courtyard,* probably in collaboration with Andrea Sansovino. In addition to the library, there are numerous works of art by artists such as: Simone Martini, Bernardo Daddi, Dosso Dossi, Filippino Lippi, Salvator Rosa, Giotto and many others.

**National Museum of Science.** Situated in the Palace in Piazza Castellani, on the left side of the Uffizi. A severe three story building with solid round arched windows, and made of rusticated stone, from 1574 to 1841, it was the seat of the Justices of the "Rota". Restored from 1888 to 1930, it became the seat of the only Scientific Museum in Italy, and later the seat of the "Crusca Academy", for the study of the Italian Language. Among the numerous and important instruments from the Medici collections and private gifts, are rare instruments invented by Galileo Galilei.

**Museum of Anthropology and Ethnology.** Founded by Mantegazza (1869), it is located in the Palazzo Non Finito (unfinished Palace - on Via del Proconsolo 12), so-called because it was left unfinished by Buontalenti who began its construction in 1593 for Alessandro Strozzi.

**Museum of Zoology called "La Specola" (observatory).** Grand Duke Pietro Leopoldo (1779) bought the old Torrigiani Palace and destined it to house the *Astronomical Observatory* and the *Tribune of Galileo Galilei.* It is a unique museum in Italy because of its botanical, zoological, anatomical and mineralogical collections.

**Topographical Museum of "Florence as it was".** This is located near the Cathedral opposite to the Hospital of Santa Maria Nuova and has a beautiful portico by Buontalenti. The entrance to the Museum is on Via dell'Oriuolo where at one time, was the convent of the Oblate Nuns. Its splendid rooms were restored to their original state and it contains a rich, ample photographic and pictorial documentation that allows the visitor to get an idea of the monuments and aspect of the Florence of yesterday.

**Convent of Santa Maria Maddalena dei Pazzi.** In the *Chapter room* of this convent (Borgo Pinti 58) is the famous triptych frescoed by Perugino. For the visit ring at the house of the custodian at N. 7 or contact the custodian of the High School at N. 5. Here the artist painted the *Crucifixion* (1493-96), that occupies the entire wall and is divided into three arches. In the center *Christ Crucified* with *Mary Magdalen;* on the sides; *St. Bernard, the Madonna, St. John the Evangelist* and *St. Benedict* immersed in profound and human resignation. The chiaroscuro effects are magnificent and in the background is a wide and splendid Umbrian landscape. Farther ahead to the right, on Via Farini is the

**Sinagogue.** (Monumental plan N. 25), built by Micheli and Treves between 1872-74 (fig. 192), it is advisable to visit at sunset in order better to admire the Moorish style and decoration. For the visit contact the custodian in charge; if the gate is closed, pass through the small gate on the right.

**Chiostro dello Scalzo** (Via Cavour, N. 69, near Piazza San Marco next to the Buontalenti Palace, now seat of the Court of Appeal). Ring for the custodian in order to visit the graceful *"Chiostro dello Scalzo"* (seat of the Confraternity of St. John the Baptist, called "dello Scalzo" because in a procession, the cross-bearer walked barefooted). On the walls, painted in chiaro-scuro, are *Episodes in the life of St. John the Baptist* by Andrea del Sarto (1515-25), and continued by Franciabigio in the period when the artist was in Paris.

**Coenaculum of the Convent of Sant'Apollonia** (Via XVII Aprile, 1 - near Piazza San Marco. Monumental plan N. 6 - contact custodian). The building presently hosts the University for Foreigners and the student cafeteria, and headquarters of the Museum of Andrea del Castagno, by whom is the fresco of the *Last Supper* (1450), famous for its bold and dramatic realism.

**Fig. 192 - The Synagogue**

**Coenaculum of the Convent of Foligno.** By ringing the custodian of Via Faenza, 42 we can admire the Refectory of the ex-Convent of the Franciscans in which there is a *Last Supper* by Perugino, brought to light in 1895 but still discussed stylistically. Leaving here and reaching Via Nazionale, opposite Via dell'Ariento (animated street of the Central Market), observe the beautiful *Tabernacle with Madonna and Saints* in glazed terra-cotta by Giovanni Della Robbia (1522).

**Coenaculum of San Salvi.** (Belonging to the old Abbey of the Vallombrosian Monks). Located on Via San Salvi N. 16 - Plan N. 42. Among the works of Andrea del Sarto this *Last Supper* is admired for its design, color and formal rendering of *Christ* and the *Apostles,* and is considered the greatest masterpiece of this artist, considered "without errors". Among other works is the fragment of the *Monument to St. Giovanni Gualberto* by Benedetto da Rovezzano and the important gallery of plaster casts of Lorenzo Bartolini. To the visitor with an automobile we suggest seeing the nearby

**Stadium** (plan N. 44), in the vast Campo di Marte with entrance on Viale Manfredo Fanti. (If closed, ring for the custodian). It is a bold work in reinforced concrete by Pier Luigi Nervi (1932).

**Pools.** Now located in all outskirts of the city.

**Castle of Vincigliata.** As shown on the monumental map (N. 41), with our own means we reach the Ponte a Mensola, where on the left, among the green cypresses we see the Villa "I Tatti" once owned by the American art historian Berenson who willed it to Harvard University. Continuing upwards among the picturesque hills of Fiesole and Settignano, we reach the famous Castle of Vincigliata. Although it is not possible to visit because it is private property, this excursion is particularly interesting for the pleasantness of the woods of pine and cypress trees that surround the Castle. Farther ahead, arriving at the fork for Fiesole, turning to the right, we descend to the nearby picturesque town of Settignano. (plan N.40); bus n.10 from Piazza S. Marco.

**Settignano.** This was the cradle of great artists like Desiderio da Settignano, the Rossellino and da Maiano brothers. After Settignano, on the right the picturesque Via Rossellino, winding through a marvellous landscape of olive groves and cypresses, we arrive at the "Villa Gamberaria" belonging to Rossellino, whose famous Italian garden ispired the "Longwood garden" in Pennsylvania.

**Fortress Belvedere,** located on the hill overlooking the Boboli gardens (monumental plan N. 46 - fig. 193). Take bus N. 13 to the Caffé Fontana, from where, walking along the picturesque Via S. Leonardo, we reach the Porta S. Giorgio on the left of which is the entrance to the Fortress (1590-95). A splendid example of a military fortress, it was built by Bernardo Buontalenti, who erected it on the bastions of the Porta San Giorgio on order of Ferdinand I Medici. Ex-military barracks, it was opportunely restored and is used for art expositions and other tourist manifestations. Even if the Fortress is closed, one can always go to the vast terrace to admire the magnificent panoramic view of the city.

**Fortress da Basso.** Located on Viale Filippo Strozzi (monumental plan N. 48), near the Central Railway Station. Called "da Basso" (lower) because of its position. It was built following a design by Antonio Sangallo for Alessandro dei Medici (1530), when he became first Duke of Florence. It is now head expositive.

**Russian Orthodox Church.** Located on Via Leone X, N. 8, East of the Fortress da Basso (plan N. 48). It is easily recognizable because of its small green and gilded cupolas.

Fig. 193 - The Fortress Belvedere

**Monastery of the Certosa.** Built in a suggestive location at the doors of the picturesque countryside of Chianti (fig. 194). Bus N. 31 from Piazza S. Maria Novella: distance 6 km. from the city. It was founded by Niccolò Acciaioli (1310), Grand Seneschal of the King of Naples and Viceroy of Apulia. The monastery is unique in Italy because of its particular position, its architecture and the disposition of the cells. Recently, radical restorations have been made in the large halls, where numerous works of art and the celebrated frescoes by Pontormo, have been placed. The Carthusians, now reduced to a few monks, have been substituted by the Cistercians who accompany the visitors illustrating the works of art.

**Florentine and Medicean Villas.** Anyone wishing to partecipate in the organized visits held in Spring and Summer, can consult any travel agency or his own hotel director. These sources have information about the visits and also about all the manifestations of art and folklore.

**Stibbert Villa or Museum.** Located North of the city in the picturesque hillside of Montughi (3 km. from the center). Bus N. 1 from Via Cerretani which stops on Via Vittorio Emanuele II, in front of Villa Fabbricotti, residence of Queen Victoria of England during her second trip to Florence. Farther ahead to the right is Via Stibbert leading to the villa which houses the Stibbert Museum, willed to the city of Florence in 1906 by the collector Frederick Stibbert. It contains a vast collection of costumes, jewellery, furniture, and furnishings and is enriched by the celebrated Cavalcade, made up of 14 armed cavaliers wearing XVI cent. costumes. The visit is accompanied by the personnel of the Museum. After the tour the visitor can relax in the splendid park.

**Cascine Park.** Bus N. 17 (see plan N. 29). This splendid park, formerly the home of the Grand Ducal families, was opened to the public in the XVIII century. The ample park stretches lengthwise along the Arno up to the confluence with the Mugnone. It is very relaxing and especially suited for strolls and gatherings. Among the local festivals held here we mention the "Festa del grillo" (of the cricket), which takes place on Ascension day. There are also many sports facilities (hippodrome, tennis courts, pools).

In the middle of the park, on the right of the large square is the School of Forestry and Agrarian Sciences. Ahead is the small zoo and the School of Aeronautics. The park ends with the *bust* of the Indian Prince Rajarama Cuttraputi (fig. 195), who died in Florence in 1870 at 20 years

Fig. 194

**Fig. 195 - Cascine Park - Monument to an Indian Prince**

of age. This small monument by Fuller is popularly called "Indiano", and commemorates the place where the young prince was cremated. Not being able to disperse the ashes in the Ganges, they were scattered at the point where the Arno meets the Mugnone.

An excursion to this park is particularly recommended as a conclusion of a visit to Florence. The vision of the numerous and incomparable works of art seen, finds a worthy cornice in the green of this magnificent park.

# INDEX OF THE MAIN ARTISTS

Paolo Uccello (Paolo di Dono) (1397-1475).

Parigi, Alfonso (XVI sec.).

Parmigianino (Francesco Mazzola) (1503-1540).

Perugino (Pietro Vannucci) (1445-1523).

Piazzetta, Giovanni Battista (1682-1754).

Piero della Francesca (m. 1492).

Piero di Cosimo (1462-1521).

Pino, Paolo (XVI sec.).

Pollaiolo Antonio (Antonio Benci) (1433-1498).

Pollaiolo, Piero Benci) (1443-96).

Pontormo (Jacopo Carrucci) (1494-1557).

Rubens, Pietre Paul (1577-1640).

Ruysdael, Jacob van (1626-82).

Reni, Guido (1585-1642).

Rigaud, Hyacinthe (1659-1743).

Rosso Fiorentino (Giovanni Battista di Jacopo) (1494-1541).

Raffaello, Sanzio (1483-1520).

Rembrandt, Harmenzoon van Rijn (1606-69).

Savoldo, Girolamo (c. 1480 - c. 1548).

Sebastiano del Piombo (Sebastiano Luciani) (1485-1547).

Signorelli, Luca (1411-1523).

Sodoma (Giovanni Antonio Bazzi) (1477-1549).

Sustermans, Justus (1597-1681).

Tintoretto, Domenico (Domenico Robusti) (1562-1637).

Tintoretto, Jacopo (Jacopo Robusti) (1518-1594).

Tura, Cosmè (1520-1595).

Titian (Tiziano Vecelio) (1490-1576).

Van Dyck, Anthony (1599-1641).

Vasari, Giorgio (1511-74).

Veronese (Paolo Caliari) (1528-88).

Verrocchio, Andrea del (Andrea di Cione) (1435-88).

Weyden, Rogier van der (1399-1464).

# USEFUL INFORMATION

**Emergency Calls**

Police: Emergency 113
Carabineers: Emergency 112
City Police: Emergency 35 21 41
Fire Brigade: Emergency 115
Railway Police: (Central Station) 21 22 96
Traffic Police: 57 77 77
ACI (Road Patrols) Italian Automobile Club 116
Florence Police Headquarters 4 97 71
Prefecture 2 78 31
Magistrate's Court: 26 42 71

**Ambulance**

Clearing Centre. Calls for the "Loggetta" zone: 49 76
"Misericordia" (Ambulance with doctor on board 24 hr) 21 22 22
"Fratellanza Militare" (Ambulance with doctor on board 24 hr.) 21 55 55
CRI (Italian Red Cross) 2 15 38
UCM (Mobile Coronary Unit) 21 44 44

**First Aid**

Medical First Aid: 47 78 91
Emergency Obstetrician: 43 99 366
Drug Addiction Service: 48 30 10

**Hospitals**

Citizens of the EEC have the right to the same assistance and the same facilities as Italian citizens, on presentation of Form E 111, which can be obtained in their own respective Countries from the Social Security Offices. (In Italy - USL Iffices).

General Hospital of Careggi, 85, Viale Morgagni. Tel. 4 39 91. First Aid Post: 4 39 92 35
Arcispedale of Santa Maria Nuova, 1, Piazza S. Maria Nuova. Tel. 2 75 81 (First Aid Post: Tel. 2 75 81)
Anna Meyer Paediatrics Hosp., 13, Via L. Giordano. Tel. 43 99 1 (First Aid Post: 4 39 97 21)
I.O.T. Tuscan Orthopaedic Institute, 41, Viale Michelangelo. Tel. 2 76 91
C.T.O. Orthopaedic Traumatological Centre. 1, Lg. P. Palagi. Tel. 41 36 45
Nuovo San Giovanni di Dio. 3, Via Torregalli. Tel. 2 76 61
Santa Maria Annunciata Hosp. Via dell'Antella. Tel. 2 79 41
Camerata Hospital. 68, Via della Piazzola. Tel. 57 74 64
Sant'Antonino Hospital. 6, Via Vecchia Fiesolana, Fiesole. Tel. 59 96 22
Florentine Ophthalmic. Hosp.. 213, Via Masaccio. Tel. 57 84 44

**Pharmacies in the Centre - Open 24 hours**

In addition to medicines and sanitary articles the pharmacies also sell a complete range of baby products and foods (powdered homogenised milk, etc.). Blood pressure can be measured also in the pharmacies.

For information and open times; Tel. 192

All'Insegna del Moro, 20/R, Piazza San Giovanni. Tel. 21 13 43
Comunale Pharmacy N° 13, Inside the Central Railway Station. Tel. 26 34 35
Molteni. 7/R, Via Calzaioli. Tel. 26 34 90

**Lost Property**

All objects lost in the town area, including those handed to the Police or Carabineers, are delivered to the Lost Property Office (Ufficio Oggetti Smarriti) where they can be collected every day (except Thursday) from 9.00 to 12.00.

Lost Property Office, Via Circondaria. Tel. 36 79 43.

**Impounded Cars Park**

Parco Auto Requisite. 19, Via Circondaria. Tel. 35 15 62

**Reporting Thefts**

All reports of theft of documents, currency, (or other); can be made at all Police or Carabineer Stations.

Central Police Headquarters: 2, Via Zara. Tel. 4 97 71
Carabineers. 48, Via Borgognissanti. Tel. 21 21 21

**Post and Telegraph Offices**

Post & Telegraph Office - Information and Claims: 53/55, Via Pietrapiana. Tel. 21 79 41
Telephonic Information: Tel. 160

**National Telephones**

Acceptance: Palazzo delle Poste, Via Pellicceria. Tel. 21 41 45
Operator Services: 15 European Countries. 170 Extra European Countries

**Tourist Information**

Consortium, Italian Tourist Association (Consorzio I.T.A.). Administration, 9/A Viale Gramsci. Tel. 247 82 31 (8-13/15-18.00)
Tourist Office, Inside S. Maria Novella Station. Tel. 28 28 93 / 28 35 00 / 21 95 37 (Hours 8.40-20.30)
Fortezza da Basso; Tourist Bus Terminal. Tel. 47 19 60 (10.30-14 / 15-19.30) Easter to 7 November.
Airport Terminal, S. Maria Novella Station, Platform 5. Tel. 21 60 73 (Hours 7.00-20.00).

**Motorways Information Points**

AGIP Service Area "Peretola Sud". (A 11) Tel. 421 18 00 / 421 18 02 (8.40-20.30)
IP Service Area "Chianti Est" (A 1) Tel. 62 13 49 (10.30-14 / 15-19.30) Easter to 7 November

Provincial Tourist Office (Ente Provinciale per il Turismo, Via Manzoni 16. Tel. 247 81 41/5.
Autonomous Tourist Organization (Azienda Autonoma di Turismo, Via Tornabuoni, 15. Tel. 21 65 44/45.

**IMPORTANT:**

A complete list of up-dated prices of Hotels, Boarding Houses, Camping Sites, etc. is available, free, from all Tourist and Hotel Information Offices.

**Hotel Reservations**

Florence Promhotels. 72 Viale Volta. Tel. 57 04 81
Coopal. 2R Via il Prato. Tel. 21 95 25
C.R.A.T. Regional Consortium of Tourist Companies of Tuscany, 5, Via Martelli Tel. 29 49 00. (Written reservations only)
Toscana Hotels 80. 9/A Viale Gramsci. Tel. 247 85 43/4/5

**Guided Tours by Motor Coach**

Tours of the City:  **Morning Visit "Itinerary A"**
Departure and arrival Piazza dell'Unità (9.20-12.30)
Cathedral of Santa Maria del Fiore (Duomo), Giotto's
Campanile (Belltower), Baptistery, Academy
Gallery (David), Piazzale Michelangelo, Piazza Pitti, Boboli Gardens, Palatine Gallery.

**Afternoon Visit "Itinerary B"**

Departure and arrival Piazza dell'Unità (14.20-18.00)
Piazza della Signoria, Palazzo Vecchio, Loggia de' Lanzi, Uffizi Gallery, Fiesole, Santa Croce.

Excursions to Pisa:  **Afternoon Visit to Pisa**
Daily from March 16 to October 31 with departure in Piazza dell'Unità (14.30-19.15) and from November 1 to March 15, only on Tuesday, Thursday, Saturday and Sunday, with departure from Piazza dell'Unità at 14.00 hours.

Excursions to Siena
and San Gimignano:  **Visit to Siena and San Gimignano**
Daily from March 16 to October 31 with departure and arrival in Piazza dell'Unità (9.00-18.00) and from November 1 to March 15 only on Monday, Wednesday and Friday.

Excursions to the Gardens
of Florentine Villas:  **Afternoon Visits to Gardens of Florentine Villas**
Departure from Piazza S. Maria Novella at 14.15 only on Tuesday, Thursday, Saturday from April 7 to June 30.

For further information and bookings apply to the local Travel Agencies.

**Tourist Guides**

Official Tourist Guides "Coop. GIOTTO"
9/A Viale Gramsci Tel. 247 81 88 (Authorized Guides for individual and Group visits).

**Public Transport Information**

Radio Taxi: 4390/4798
ATAF (Florence Bus Service (Autolinee Fiorentine) 57/R Piazza Duomo. Information Tel. 21 23 01
CAP (Services with Neighbouring Towns) Piazza Stazione. Tel. 21 46 37 / 29 42 05
CAT (Services with Neighbouring Towns) 5/R Via Fume. Tel. 28 34 00
COPIT (Services with Neighbouring Towns) 22/R Piazza S.M.Novella. Tel. 21 54 51
LAZZI (Services with Neighbouring Towns) 4 Piazza Stazione. Tel. 28 38 78 / 21 51 54
SITA (Services with Neighbouring Towns) 15 Via S. Caterina da Siena. Tel. 28 46 61 / 21 47 21
FFSS (National Railways) Information, Train Times. Inside S. Maria Novella Station. Tel. 27 87 85

**Automobile Hire** (For further information see Yellow Pages under "Autonoleggi")

AVIS, 128/R, Borgonissanti. Tel. 21 36 29
BUDGET Rent a Car. 113 Borgognissanti. Tel. 29 30 21
EUROPCAR, 53-55/R Via Borgognissanti. Tel. 29 34 44
HERTZ, 33 Via M. Finiguerra. Tel. 28 22 60
MAGGIORE, 33 Via M. Finiguerra. Tel. 21 02 38
EURODRIVE, 7R Via Alamanni. Tel. 29 86 39
INTERRENT, 133a Borgongissanti. Tel. 21 86 65

## Motorbike, Scooter and Bicycle Hire

FREE MOTOR, 6/R Via S. Monaca. Tel. 29 51 02
MOTORENT. 9/R Via S. Zanobi. Tel. 49 01 13
CIAO & BASTA. Via Alamanni (underneath the Central Station) Tel. 21 33 07
PROGRAM. 135/R Borgognissanti. Tel. 28 29 16
SKATEBIKE, 70R Viale dei Mille. Tel. 57 14 78
CIAO RENT SABRA, 8, Via Degli Artisti. Tel. 57 62 56
VESPA RENT, 103R, Via Pisana. Tel. 71 56 91
EURODRIVE, 48R, Via Della Scala. Tel. 29 86 39

## Airports

Air Terminal of Consortium ITA: Inside S. Maria Novella Station. Hours: 7.00-20.00

Passengers leaving Florence on flights from Pisa Airport "Galileo Galilei" may book in and register baggage at the Air Terminal, in the main station S. Maria Novella, and obtain their embarkation cards. Direct connection with the Airport is ensured by trains departing every hour.

Civil Airport of Peretola, 1, Via del Termine. Tel. 37 01 23
Pisa Airport "Galileo Galilei". Tel. 050/2 80 88

## Airline Companies (For further information see Yellow Pages)

Alitalia Firenze, 10/R Lungarno Acciaiuoli. Tel. 2 78 88/9
Air France, 9 Borgo SS Apostoli. Tel. 21 83 55
British Airways, 36/R Via Vigna Nuova. Tel. 21 86 55
Iberia, 2 Piazza Antinori. Tel. 21 52 27
Lufthansa, 6, Via Pellicceria. Tel. 26 28 90/7
Swissair, 1 Via del Parione. Tel. 29 50 55
Thai Airlines, 4 Via dei Conti. Tel. 29 43 72
TWA, 2/R Piazza S. Trinità. Tel. 29 68 56

## Travel Agencies (For further information see Yellow Pages)

ABC. 23-25-27/R Via dei banchi. Tel. 28 38 25
American Express Company, 49/R Via Guicciardini. Tel. 27 87 51
Arno Travel Service. 7/R Piazza Ottaviani. Tel. 21 99 88/29 52 51
CIT. 56/R Via cavour. Tel. 29 43 06 - 51/R Piazza Stazione. Tel. 28 41 45
Eyre & Humbert. 56R Via del Parione. Tel. 26 22 51
Globus. 2/R Piazza S. Trinità. Tel. 21 49 92
Melia'. 63/R Via Cavour. Tel. 21 91 90
New Tours. 20/A Via G. Monaco. Tel. 32 11 55
Roller Tour. 23/R Piazza Stazione. Tel. 21 17 38
Universalturismo. 7/R Via degli Speziali. Tel. 21 72 41
Wagon-Lits Turismo. 27/R Via del Giglio. Tel. 21 88 51
World Vision Travel. 4 Lungarno Acciaiuoli. Tel. 29 52 71

## Consular Visas (Procedures)

Agenzia Piana. 75 int. Via R. Giuliani. Tel. 437 94 39

## Consulates

Austria. 9 Via dei Servi. Tel. 21 53 52
Belgium. 4 Via dei Conti. Tel. 28 20 94
Bolivia. 24 Via Torre del Gallo. Tel. 22 00 17
Chile. 25 Via L. Alamanni. Tel. 21 41 31
Columbia. 19 Scali Manzoni, Livorno. Tel. 0586/ 3 52 95
Cost Rica. 10 Via Giambologna. Tel. 57 36 03
Denmark. 13 Via dei Servi. Tel. 21 20 07
Dominican Republic. 27 Via Ricasoli. Tel. 21 48 46
France. 2 Piazza Ognissanti. Tel. 21 35 09
Finland. 6 Via Strozzi. Tel. 29 32 38
Federal Germany. 22 Borgo SS. Apostoli. Tel. 29 47 22
Great Britain. 2 Lungarno Corsini. Tel. 28 41 33
Greece. 19 Largo Attias, Livorno. Tel. 0586/81 00 79
Haiti. 2 Via Cerretani. Tel. 28 26 83
Holland. 81 Via Cavour. Tel. 47 52 49
Honduras. 30 Via dei Bardi. Tel. 28 22 19
Malta. 42 Viale Gramsci. Tel. 24 29 58
Norway. 2, Via Cerretani. Tel. 228 03 13
Panama. 8 Via Respighi. Tel. 35 14 93
Peru. 17 Via della Mattonaia. Tel. 67 23 45
Portugal. 35 Via S. Reparata. Tel. 21 59 59
Salvador. 17 Via Fra' D. Bonvicini. 57 97 31
Spain. 21 Via G. La Pira. Tel. 21 05 59
Sweden. 4 Via della Scala. Tel. 29 68 65
Switzerland. 5 Piazzale Galileo. Tel. 22 24 34
United States of America. 38 Lungarno Vespucci. Tel. 29 82 76
Venezuela. 10 Via Giambologna. Tel. 58 80 82

**Privates Garages** (Central Zone)

Alfieri. 8 Via Alfieri. Tel. 247 77 91
Anglo-American. 5 Via Barbadori. Tel. 21 44 18/21 86 04
Autofficina Aemme. 47 Viale Don Minzone. Tel. 57 60 71
Bargello 170/R Via Ghibellina. Tel. 28 70 58
Bindi. 1/B Viale Matteotti. Tel. 57 99 06
Centrale. 50/R Via dei Fossi. Tel. 21 00 18
Ciclop. 2 Via S. Orsola. Tel. 28 77 11
D'Azeglio. 1/R Via Alfieri. Tel. 247 77 57
Del Centro. 38-39/R Piazza Duomo. Tel. 21 66 72
Delle Nazioni. 37/R Via Alamanni. Tel. 28 28 14
Dugini D. 47/R Via delle Terme. Tel. 29 41 69
Duomo. 44/R Via Oriuolo. Tel. 234 04 94
Europa. 96 Borgo Ognissanti. Tel. 26 23 56/21 39 53
Faenza. 46/R Via Faenza. Tel. 28 46 85
Far. 101 Via San Gallo. Tel. 48 34 10
F. Fei. 14-16/R Via Presto di S. Martino. Tel. 29 46 92
Ferrucci. 15/R Lungarno Ferrucci. Tel. 681 16 50
Garage Zanobi. 29 Via S. Zanobi. Tel. 48 93 63
GE.GA.FI. 94 Via Palazzuolo. Tel. 21 92 16/29 61 37
Giglio. 24/R Via Giglio. Tel. 21 61 52
Inferno. 9/R Via Inferno. Tel. 21 09 70
International Garage. 29 Via Palazzuolo. Tel. 28 23 86
La Farina. 26/R Via La Farina. Tel. 24 28 10
La Stazione. 3/A Via Alamanni. Tel. 28 47 68/28 48 68
Luna. 41/R Via Panicale. Tel. 29 40 44
Lungarno. 10 Borgo S. Jacopo. Tel. 28 25 42
Mario. 1/R Piazza Crocifisso. Tel. 29 22 50
Masini. 11/R Via Agli. Tel. 21 25 78
Mercatelli. 13/R Via S. Antonino. Tel. 21 04 90
Nazionale. 21 Via Nazionale. Tel. 28 40 41
Piccione B. 19 1/R Borgo Pinti. Tel. 247 76 77
Ponte Vecchio, 35-45/R Via dei Bardi. Tel. 29 86 00
Santa Reparata di Galluzzo G. 12/e/f/g Via S. Reparata. Tel. 47 38 42
Sole. 14/R Via Sole. Tel. 26 16 95
Sport. 82/R Via S. Gallo. Tel. 48 33 83
Supergarage. 19 Via Fiesolana. Tel. 247 78 71
Verdi. 13/R Via G. da Verrazzano. Tel. 24 49 21
Vettori. 4/R Piazza Vettori. Tel. 22 56 02

**Swimming Pools**

Bellariva "G. Nannini". 6 Lungarno Colombo. Tel. 67 75 21
Costoli. Viale Paoli. Tel. 67 57 44
Le Pavoniere. Viale degli Olmi. Tele. 36 75 06

**Sports Grounds, Stadium, etc.**

Municipal Stadium. Viale M. Fanti
"Palagiglio" Palace of Sport. Viale Paoli.
Visarno Race-course (Gallops) Parco delle Cascine. Tel. 36 05 98
Mulina Race-course (Trotting) Parco delle Cascine. Te. 41 79 72
Ugolino Golf Course. Via Chiantigiana. Grassina. (10 km from Florence). Tel. 230 10 09
Tennis Club. Parco delle Cascine, Viale Visarno. Tel. 35 66 51

**Advance Booking - Shows - Concerts - Theatres**

Box Office. 10/A/R Via della Pergola. Timetable: 10.00-20.00. Tel. 24 23 61/24 18 81

**Camping Grounds and Hostels**

Camping Villa Camerata. 2/A Viale Righi. Tel. 61 03 00
Camping Autosole. Outlet N° 19 from Motorway "Autostrada del Sole" Calenzano. Tel. 88 23 91
Campeggio (Camping) Panoramico. Via Peramonda, Fiesole. Tel. 59 90 69
Camping for Italians & Foreigners (Campeggio Italiani & Stranieri). 80 Viale Michelangelo. Tel. 681 19 77
Camping Internazionale Firenze. 2 Via S. Cristoforo, Bottai. Tel. 203 47 04
Camping (Campeggio) Mugello Verde. Loc. La Fortezza, S. Piero a Sieve. Tel. 84 85 11
Villa Camerata Hostel. 2/4 Viale Righi. Tel. 60 14 51
S. Monaca Hostel. 6 Via S. Monaca. Tel. 26 83 38

## SPECIAL EVENTS IN FLORENCE

### January

Opera/Symphony Season (Municipal Theatre) Teatro Comunale
Drama Season (Pergola Theatre)
Pitti Fashion Shows - Man (Uomo) - Child (Bimbo) -
Household (Casa) - Lingerie
The Italian Man (Uomo Italia)
Children's Fashion (Moda Bimbo)
Epifania

242

### February

Opera/Symphony Season
Drama Season
Pitti Yarns
Italcaravan Turisport

Carneval

### March

Drama Season
Florence at the Table (Fortezza da Basso)
Prato Expo

### March/April

Explosion of the Cart (Scoppio del Carro ) (Easter Sunday)
Easter

### April

Drama Season
International Craftwork Exhibition (Fortezza del Basso)
Garden Show (Fortezza da Basso)
Flower Show (Piazza Signoria)

### May

Opera/Symphony Season - Music Festival (Maggio Musicale)
Florentia Auxilia (Fortezza da Basso)
Festa del Grillo - Ascension (Parco delle Cascine)

### June

Opera/Symphony Season - Music Festival (Maggio Musicale)
Pitti Uomo (Men's Fashions)
Uomo Italia (Men's Fashions)
Feast of St. John (San Giovanni) (Fireworks)
Football in costume
Fiesole Summer (Estate Fiesolana) (music, cinema, and other shows)
Corpus Christi (Procession)

### July

Pitti Bimbo (Children's Fashions)
Moda Bimbo (Children's Fashions)
Fiesole Summer (Estate Fiesolana)
Florence Summer (Firenze Estate) (Various shows)
Cinema at Night (Forte Belvedere)

### August

Fiesole Summer (Estate Fiesolana)
Florence Summer (Firenze Estate)
Cinema at Night (Forte Belvedere)

### September

Fiesole Summer (Estate Fiesolana)
Florence Summer (Estate Firenze)
Cinema at Night (Forte Belvedere)
Florence Gift Mart
Pitti Yarns (Pitti Filati)
Bird Exhibition (Fiera degli Uccelli) (Porta Romana)
Paper Lantern Festival (Festa della rificolona)

### September/October

Biennial Antiques Exhibition (Palazzo Strozzi)

### October

Herbalist (Fortezza da Basso)
AIPO Show Fishing (Fortezza da Basso)
RIAF - HI-Fi (Fortezza da Basso)
Drama Season (Pergola Theatre)

### November

Opera/Sympony Season (Municipal Theatre) (Teatro Comunale)
Drama Season
The Leather Line (Linea Pelle) (Fortezza da Basso)

### December

Opera/Symphony Season
Drama Season
Christmas.

### Business Hours

### Banks and Credit Institutes

08.20 - 13.20 From Monday to Friday
14.45 - 15.45 (excluding Friday afternoon)

### Shops (indicative)

Summer: 9-13 / 16-20 (Closed Saturday afternoon and Sunday)
Winter: 9-13 / 15.30-19.30 (closed Monday morning)


### USEFUL INFORMATION

Museums, Galleries, and Private Foundations.

State Apartments (Pitti Palace)
(Appartamenti Monumentali (Palazzo Pitti)
Piazza Pitti Tel. 21 03 23
Visiting hours— Weekdays 9-14 Holidays 9-13
Closed: Monday

Library of the Maggiore Seminary
(Biblioteca del Seminario Maggiore)
Lungarno Soderini, 19 Tel. 28 38 75

Medici-Laurentian Library
(Biblioteca Medicea-Laurenziana)
Piazza San Lorenzo, 9 Tel. 21 07 60
Visiting hours: 9-17
Closed: Sunday and Holidays

Riccardi Library
(Biblioteca Riccardiana)
Via de' Ginori, 14 Tel. 21 56 86
Visiting hours: 11-13
Closed: Sunday and Holidays

Medici Chapels
(Cappelle Medicee)
Piazza Madonna degli Aldobrandini Tel. 21 32 06
Visiting hours: Weekdays 9-14 Holidays 9-13
Closed: Monday

The House of Dante
(Casa di Dante)
Via Santa Margherita, 1 Tel. 28 33 43
Visiting hours: Weekdays 9-12.30 / 15-18.30
                          Holidays 9-12.30
Closed: Wednesday

The House of Michelangelo Buonarroti
(Casa di Michelangelo Buonarroti)
Via Ghibellina, 70 Tel. 24 17 52
Visiting hours: Weekdays 10-14 Holidays 9-13
Closed: Tuesday

Last Supper by Ghirlandaio at All Saints' Church
(Cenacolo del Ghirlandaio a Ognissanti)
Borgognissanti, 42 Tel. 29 68 02
Visiting hours: Weekdays 9-12 / 16-18
Closed: Sunday and Holidays

Last Supper by Perugino
(Cenacolo del Perugino)
Conservatorio di Foligno
Via Faenza, 42 Tel. 28 69 82

Last Supper by Andrea del Castagno in the Monastery of Sant'Apollonia
(Cenacolo di Andrea del Castagno a Sant'Apollonia)
Via 27 Aprile, 1 Tel. 28 70 74
Visiting hours: Weekdays Holidays 9-13
Closed: Monday

Last Supper by Andrea del Sarto at the Convent of San Salvi
(Cenacolo di Andrea del Sarto a San Salvi)
Via San Salvi, 16 Tel. 67 75 70
Visiting hours: Weekdays 9-14 Holidays 9-13
Closed: Monday

The Last Supper of the Church of Santa Maria del Carmine and the Brancacci Chapel
(Cenacolo di Santa Maria del Carmine e Cappella Brancacci)
Piazza del Carmine Tel. 21 23 31

The Last Supper of the Church of the Holy Spirit and Roman Foundation
(Cenacolo di Santo Spirito e Fondazione Romana)
Piazza Santo Spirito, 29 Tel. 28 70 43
Visiting hours: Weekdays 9-14 Holidays 8-13
Closed: Monday

Cloister of the Barefooted Friar
(Chiostro dello Scalzo)
Via Cavour, 69 Tel. 48 48 08
Visiting hours: 9-13
Ring the bell.

Contini-Bonacossi Collection (Pitti Palace)
(Collezione Contini-Bonacossi (Palazzo Pitti)
Palazzina della Meridiana. Boboli Gardens
Visiting hours: 10.00 (Only by arrangement - Uffizi Gallery Sec.)
Closed: Mon. Wed. Fri. and Holidays

Complex of St. Mary of the Flower (Cathedral)
Complesso Santa Maria del Fiore "Duomo"
Piazza del Duomo Tel. 21 32 29
Brunelleschi's Dome
Visiting hours: 10-17
Closed: Sunday

Baptistery
Visiting hours: 10-17

Crypt of Santa Reparata
Visiting hours: 10-17

Giotto's Campanile
Visiting hours: 9-17 Winter 9-19 Summer

Cricifixion by Perugino
(Crocefissione del Perugino)
Borgo Pinti, 58 Tel. 247 84 20
Visiting hours: 9-12 / 17-19

Michelucci Foundation
(Fondazione Michelucci)
Via Fra G. Angelico, 15 Tel. 59 71 49
Fiesole

Drawings and Prints Cabinet
(Gabinetto Disegni e Stampe)
Viale Giovine Italia, 6

Corsini Gallery (Corsini Palace)
(Galleria Corsini (Palazzo Corsini))
Via del Parione, 11 Tel. 28 76 29
Visited only by appointment

Uffizi Gallery
(Galleria degli Uffizi)
Loggiato degli Uffizi, 6 Tel. 21 83 41
Visiting hours: Weekdays 9-19 Holidays 9-13
Closed: Monday

Costume Gallery (Pitti Palace)
(Galleria del Costume (Palazzo Pitti)

Palazzina della Meridiana. Boboli Gardens
Visiting hours: Weekdays 9-14 Holidays 9-13
Closed: Monday Wednesday Friday.

Academy Gallery
(Galleria dell'Accademia)
Via Ricasoli, 60 Tel. 21 43 75
Visiting hours: Weekdays 9-14 Holidays 9-13
Closed: Monday

The Foundling Hospital Gallery
(Galleria dello Spedale degli Innocenti)
Piazza SS. Annunziata, 12 Tel. 24 77 95
Visiting hours: Weekdays Winter 9-14 Summer 9-19 Holidays 8-13
Closed: Wednesday

Palatine Gallery (Pitti Palace)
(Galleria Palatina (Palazzo Pitti)
Piazza Pitti Tel. 21 66 73
Visiting hours: Weekdays 9-14 Holidays 9-13
Closed: Monday

Archaeological Museum
(Museo Archeologico)
Via della Colonna, 36 Tel. 247 86 41
Visiting hours: Weekdays 9-14 Holidays 9-13
Closed: Monday

Bardini Museum and Corsi Gallery
(Museo Bardini e Galleria Corsi)
Piazza dei Mozzi, 1 Tel. 29 67 49
Visiting hours: Weekdays 9-14 Holidays 9-13
Closed: Wednesday

Botanical Museum and Tropical Herbarium
(Museo Botanico ed Erbario Tropicale)
Via La Pira, 4 Tel. 29 44 11
Visiting hours: 9-13 Mon. Wed. Fri.
Closed: July, August and September

Civic Museum and Archaeological Zone
(Museo Civico e Zona Archeologica)
Via Portigiani, 1 Tel. 5 94 77
Fiesole

Modern Art Gallery (Pitti Palace)
(Museo d'Arte Moderna (Palazzo Pitti)
Piazza Pitti Tel. 28 70 96
Visiting hours: Weekdays 9-14 Holidays 9-13
Closed: Monday

Silverware Museum (Pitti Palace)
(Museo degli Argenti (Palazzo Pitti)
Piazza Pitti Tel. 21 25 57
Visiting hours: Weekdays 9-14 Holidays 9-13
Closed: Monday

Musical Instruments Museum
(Museo degli Strumenti Musicali)
Via degli Alfani, 80 Tel. 21 05 02
During restorations the instruments can be seen, exclusively by appointment, in the Palazzo Vecchio

Plaster Models Museum
(Museo dei Gessi)
Piazzale di Porta Romana, 9 Tel. 22 05 21
Visiting hours: 8-14 by appointment
Closed: Sunday

Bigalo Museum
(Museo del Bigalo)
Piazza San Giovanni, 1

Museum of the Ancient Florentine House (Davanzati Palace)
(Museo della Casa Fiorentina Antica (Palazzo Davanzati)
Via Porta Rossa, 13 Tel. 21 65 18
Visiting hours: Weekdays 9-14 Holidays 9-13
Closed: Monday

The Museum of the Horne Foundation
(Museo della Fondazione Horne)
Via dei Benci, 6 Tel. 24 46 61

Visiting hours: 16-20 Mon. to Friday. 9-13 Saturday
Closed: Sunday

The Carriage Museum (Pitti Palace)
(Museo delle Carrozze (Palazzo Pitti)
Piazza Pitti Tel. 21 25 57

Wood Museum
(Museo del Legno)
Piazzale Edison, 11 Tel. 57 15 81
Appointments to visit by telephone
Closed: Sunday and holidays

Porcelain Museum (Pitti Palace)
(Museo delle Porcellane (Palazzo Pitti)
Palazzina del Cavaliere Tel. 28 79 76
Visiting hours: Weekdays 9-14 Holidays 9-13
Closed: Monday

Museum of the Church of the Holy Cross
(Museo dell'Opera di Santa Croce)
Piazza Santa Croce, 16 Tel. 24 46 19
Visiting hours: 9-12.30 / 15-18.30 March to September
9-12.30 / 15-17.00 October to Febrary
Closed: Wednesday

Museum of the Cathedral St. Mary of the Flower
(Museum dell'Opera di Santa Maria del Fiore)
Piazza Duomo, 9
Visiting hours: 9-18 Winter 9-20 Summer 10-13 Sunday

Museum of the Jewish Temple
(Museo del Tempio Israelitico)
Via Farini, 4 Tel. 24 12 10
Visiting hours: Sun. Thurs. 9-13, Mon. Wed. 14-17 May
to September.
Sun. Mon. Wed. 10-13 October to April.

Museum of Anthropology and Ethnology
(Museo di Antropologia ed Etnologia)
Via del Proconsolo, 12 Tel. 29 64 49
Visiting hours: 9-13 Mon. (Wed. and Fri. by appointment)

Museum of Geology and Paleontology
(Museo di Geologia e Paleontologia)
Via La Pira, 4 Tel. 26 27 11
Visiting hours: Mon. 14-18, Thurs. Sat. 9-13; 1st. Sun in
Month 9.30-12.30
Closed: July, August, September

Museum of Mineralogy and Lithology
(Museo di Minerologia e Litologia)
Via La Pira, 4 Tel. 29 68 76
Visiting hours: Weekdays 9-13 + 1st Sunday of the
Month. Wed. 15-18
Closed: July, August, September

Prehistory Museum
(Museo di Preistoria)
Via S. Egidio, 21 Tel. 29 51 59
Visiting hours: 9.30-12.30
Closed: Sunday

Museum of St. Mark (Beato Angelico)
(Museo di San Marco) (Beato Angelico)
Piazza San Marco, 1 Tel. 21 07 41
Visiting hours: Weekdays 9-14 Holidays 9-13
Closed: Monday

Museum of the History of Photography
(Museo di Storia della Fotografia)
F.lli Alinari
Palazzo Rucellai
Via della Vigna Nuova, 48 Tel. 21 33 70

Museum of the History of Science

Museum and Workshop of Semi Precious Stones
(Museo e Opificio delle Pietre Dure)
Via degli Alfani, 78 Tel. 21 01 02
Visiting: Sunday and holidays
Closed: Sunday and holiday

Marino Marini Museum
(Museo Marino Marini)
Piazza di San Pancrazio
Visiting hours: 10-18
Closed: Tunsday

National or Bargello Museum
(Museo Nazionale o del Bargello)
Via del Proconsolo, 4 Tel. 21 08 01
Visiting hours: Weekdays 9-14, Holidays 9-13
Closed: Monday

Primo Conti Museum
(Museo Primo Conti)
Villa Le Coste
Via Dupré, 18 Tel. 59 70 95
Fiesole

Stibbert Museum
(Museo Stibbert)
Via Stibbert, 26 Tel. 47 57 31
Visiting hours: Weekdays 9-14 Holidays 9-13
Closed: Thursday

Historic-Topographic Museum "Florence as it was".
(Museo Storico Topografico "Firenze com'era").
Rosai Collection
Via dell'Oriuolo, 24 Tel. 21 73 05
Visiting hours: Weekdays 9-14 Holidays 8-13
Closed: Thursday

Zoological Museum "The Observatory"
(Museo Zoologico "La Specola")
Via Romana, 17 Tel. 22 24 51
Visiting hours: 9-12.30 Tuesday. 9-12 Sunday - Zoological
15-18 Sat. Winter 14-17 - Anatomical

Botanical Garden "Giardino dei Semplici"
(Orto Botanico "Giardino dei Semplici")
Via Micheli, 3 Tel. 28 46 96
Visiting hours: 9-12

Medici-Riccardi Palace
(Palazzo Medici Riccardi)
Via Cavour, 1 Tel. 27 60
Visiting hours: Weekdays 9-12.30 / 15-17 Holidays 9-12
Closed: Wednesday

Strozzi Palace
(Palazzo Strozzi)
Piazza Strozzi Tel. 29 85 63
Visiting hours: 16-19
Closed: Tuesday, Thursday, Saturday

Museum of Santa Maria Novella (Chapel of the Spaniards, etc.)
(Museo di Santa Maria Novella (Cappella degli Spagnoli, ecc.)
Piazza Santa Maria Novella Tel. 28 21 87
Visiting hours: Weekdays 9-14, Holidays 8-13
Closed: Friday

(Museo di Storia della Scienza)
Piazza dei Giudici, 1 Tel. 29 34 93
Visiting hours: 10-13 / 14-16 Mon. to Fri. 10-13 Saturday - Winter.
10-13.30 / 16-20 Mon. Thurs. 10-13.30 Tues. Fri. Sat. - Summer
Closed: Sunday and holidays

Palazzo Vecchio and the Monumental Quarters
(Palazzo Vecchio e Quartieri Monumentali)
Piazza Signoria Tel. 2 76 81
Visiting times: 9-19 / 8-13
Closed: Saturday

Picture Gallery and Chapterhouse of Galluzzo
(Pinacoteca e Certosa del Galluzzo)
Certosa Tel. 204 92 26

Visiting hours: Summer 9-12 / 15-18 Winter 9-12 / 14.30-17
Closed: Monday

"A. della Ragione" Modern Art Collection
(Raccolta d'Arte Moderna "A. della Ragione")
Piazza della Signoria Tel. 28 30 78
Visiting hours: Weekdays 9-14 Holidays 8-13
Closed: Tuesday

© COPYRIGHT - BECOCCI - Largo Liverani - Florence
Printing: TIPOGRAFIA TOSCANA - Italy